DIARY OF A VIRTUOUS WOMAN

Journey from
Prostitution to Preaching
Whoredom to Worship

BETTIE J. RUSHER

Scribes of Eden Publishing
Detroit   Atlanta
www.scribesofeden.com

"See then that you walk circumspectly, not as fools but as wise, redeeming the time, because the day are evil.

Therefore, do not be unwise, but understand what the will of the Lord is."

Ephesians 5:15-17

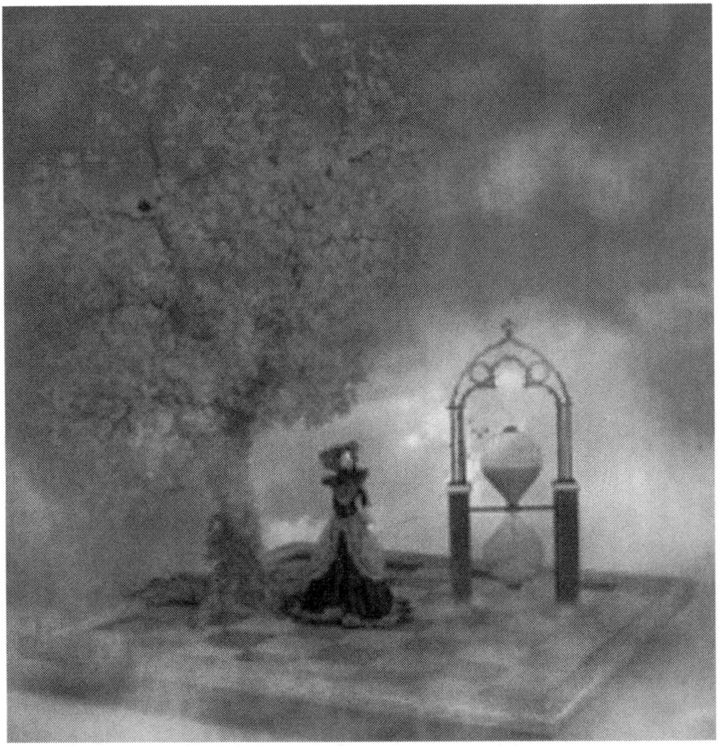

Copyright 2018 © Bettie J. Rusher

All rights reserved. This book may not be reproduced in whole or in part, by any means, without written permission of the publisher. The scanning, uploading, or electronic sharing of any part of this book constitutes unlawful piracy and theft of the author's intellectual property. If you would like to use material from the book (other than for review purposes), prior written permission must be obtained by contacting the publisher.

All Scriptures are taken from the New King James Version. Copyright © 1982 by Thomas Nelson, Inc. Used by permission. All rights reserved.

Scripture quotations marked (NLT) are taken from the Holy Bible, New Living Translation, copyright ©1996, 2004, 2007, 2013, 2015 by Tyndale House Foundation. Used by permission of Tyndale House Publishers, Inc., Carol Stream, Illinois 60188. All rights reserved.

ISBN: 9780998555515
First Edition
Printed in the United States of America

Scribes of Eden Publishing
Detroit   Atlanta
www.scribesofeden.com

Go to my website to download Free E-books,
~ *My Go-To Scriptures*
~ *31 Wisdom Keys of a Virtuous Woman*
www.backtoeden.today

The Virtuous Woman

Proverbs 31:10-31 NLT

¹⁰ Who can find a virtuous and capable wife?
   She is more precious than rubies.
¹¹ Her husband can trust her,
   and she will greatly enrich his life.
¹² She brings him good, not harm,
   all the days of her life.
¹³ She finds wool and flax
   and busily spins it.
¹⁴ She is like a merchant's ship,
   bringing her food from afar.
¹⁵ She gets up before dawn to prepare breakfast for her household
and plan the day's work for her servant girls.
¹⁶ She goes to inspect a field and buys it;
   with her earnings she plants a vineyard.
¹⁷ She is energetic and strong,
   a hard worker.
¹⁸ She makes sure her dealings are profitable;
   her lamp burns late into the night.
¹⁹ Her hands are busy spinning thread,
   her fingers twisting fiber.

[20] She extends a helping hand to the poor
   and opens her arms to the needy.
[21] She has no fear of winter for her household,
   for everyone has warm clothes.
[22] She makes her own bedspreads.
   She dresses in fine linen and purple gowns.
[23] Her husband is well known at the city gates,
   where he sits with the other civic leaders.
[24] She makes belted linen garments
   and sashes to sell to the merchants.
[25] She is clothed with strength and dignity,
   and she laughs without fear of the future.
[26] When she speaks, her words are wise,
   and she gives instructions with kindness.
[27] She carefully watches everything in her household
   and suffers nothing from laziness.
[28] Her children stand and bless her.
   Her husband praises her:
[29] "There are many virtuous and capable women in the world, but you surpass them all!"
[30] Charm is deceptive, and beauty does not last; but a woman who fears the LORD will be greatly praised.
[31] Reward her for all she has done.
   Let her deeds publicly declare her praise.

Table of Contents

The Virtuous Woman 5
Dedication 8
Preface 10
Introduction 12
Chapter 1: Back Down Memory Lane 15
Chapter 2: Checkmate 26
Chapter 3: Learning to Live the Good Life 32
Chapter 4: School of Wisdom 48
Chapter 5: School of Experience 58
Chapter 6: Prostitution to Preaching 93
Chapter 7: Whoredom to Worship 102
Chapter 8: 31 Wisdom Keys of a Virtuous Woman 106
Healing Scriptures 114
Acknowledgements 119
About the Author 120
The Sinner's Prayer 122

Dedication

I dedicate this book of my life story to my parents, William and Sadie Lowe. Even though, they aren't here in this natural realm, they are alive in my heart. There is hardly a day that I don't think about or hear their words of wisdom.

My parents loved their five children and sacrificed to provide for us.

Daddy was the sole provider, while mother was a stay at home mom. I remember my dad working very hard and wondered why mother didn't have a job to help with the household expenses. I learned that daddy didn't want her to work and she submitted to his desires.

I saw firsthand, up close the traditional family life. It wasn't perfect, but there was no doubt that we were loved by our parents. Today, as I reminisce, my heart swells up with love and appreciation for my parents who cared and protected us to the best of their ability.

My parents had high expectations of me. My being the eldest came with great responsibility. I was always reminded that I had to set a good example. Early on, I am sure that I disappointed them. I wasn't the best example for my four siblings. For many years, I was tormented by guilt and condemnation of my past. I spent many days mourning over the mistakes and wishing that I could go back in time.

Today, I have no regrets and count it all as part of Bettie's life story. I am an overcomer. I proudly share my story hoping that my life would touch all. Yes, I failed man's expectations, but God's Unconditional Love looks beyond my mistakes and failures.

Dear Mother and Daddy, I hope that you are now pleased with my life. Please, continue to watch over us from above. I look forward to the day when all separation is gone, and we all sit around the table looking into each other's eyes again.

With unconditional love, your eldest daughter, Bettie.

I hope that my life today is pleasing to my parents,
and a light to my family.
November, 2017 A.D.

Preface

As I look back at the 66 years of my life, I recall the near-death situations that I found myself in. I realize that God spared me because He has a plan for my life. Each day, I desire to live my life doing His Will.

Honestly, I wasn't very excited about the idea of sharing my diary with you, but if it's God's Will, I must be obedient. Some seasons of my life were very painful, and I would rather leave them buried. However, I am sure you will be blessed because I survived to tell you my story to help you survive. So here it is....

I was a teenager when I started writing my first diary. It was a small book with blank pages with a lock and key. Every day, I would go to my secret place where I had hidden my diary and write all of my secret thoughts. I really cherished my diary, it was my private book for my eyes only.

That is why, 50 years later, I can't believe that I am sharing my private, intimate diary. Yes, it is full of juicy stuff; my life has turned out to be very different from what I imagined and dreamed as a teenager.

I am the eldest child of five; therefore, I didn't have an older sibling to teach me the rules of life, the ropes. I learned life by going down the rough road. Truly, there are rules in this life; the quicker you learn them, the better off you will be.

In this book, you will learn Life's Game of Chess. Yes, to be a Great Chess Player, you must learn the rules and strategies. Being a Great Chess Player has nothing to do with age; some people are older than myself that still haven't learned the rules of Life's Game of Chess.

OK, I said, "Yes" to the Assignment of writing the book. Now, are you saying "Yes" to getting through this book?

Introduction

I love going to church! Why, because GOD speaks to me when I'm in His House.

One Sunday while at church, I got the revelation of the game that the enemy has played with my life. A game of chess! I can look as far back as my childhood and now recognize the different people he used to distract me from God's Will. They were pawns, knights, bishops, rooks, and finally the queen and king. Each one higher in rank and power.

Now, with this understanding, I remember one of the first pawns. As a child, we would often play the game, Hide and Seek. One of my older playmates would lure me to hide with her in a broken car in her parent's garage. She would touch me inappropriately. Years later, I learned that she openly lives a lesbian lifestyle.

But God, my King has always been there to rescue me! The exposure to that perversion could have altered my life forever. He protected me.

In my diary, I openly share very personal thoughts and encounters. I hope that you will benefit from my experiences. Perhaps, you will recognize the game of chess being played with your life and become skillful at the game. Also, to be aware that people are sent into your life for different reasons, some good and some assigned to destroy you.

The Bible says in Hosea 4:6, "*My people perish from the lack of knowledge...*" Not knowing is not an excuse in this game of life. There are consequences for being ignorant.

Please, don't miss seeing God's presence in my life throughout my journey, even sitting in that car in the garage as a child. He is always with us to deliver and protect us, even when the enemy has lured us into darkness. Learn the game of chess, to allow God to reveal His plan and strategy for your life. In reality, it is all calculated, every move and decision had a purpose.

Regardless of how you came upon this diary, I applaud you for taking the time to read it. This is the first volume; hopefully, I will have many days yet to live to tell of other adventures of my life.

My hope is that as you travel through the days of my life, you will increase in Wisdom, Knowledge, and Understanding. You have to be skillful in following God's Perfect Plan that He has predestined for you. You are victorious, not a victim.

I love this Life's Game of Chess because we have already won! Jesus has already Checkmated our enemy; the Game is Over!

Let's start our journey....

Chapter 1
Back Down Memory Lane
1979 A.D.

Here I am, 27 years old and worn out. Tired from the struggles of life. Is this all to it? There has to be more to this life; what am I doing wrong?

I was proud of the fact that every time that I was knocked down, I would always get back up, dust myself off, put on the happy face, and face the world again. Only to be knocked down; each time it would be harder to get up.

I seemed to be making mistake after mistake. I felt so lost, searching for the way out. There must be a better way to life than this for me. I was determined to live up to my potential. I wasn't born to live like this. I deserved better, I would tell myself. Why is it that I feel so unloved and unwanted? What's wrong with me?

I found myself doing things that I was totally ashamed of. I had so many secrets that only God and I knew about. I couldn't tell anyone that I had stooped so low.

Yet, when you saw me, I was dressed, and of course, smelling good. The best perfumes and make-up. Diamond watch, jewelry, and shiny new sports car.

Oh yeah, a size 5/6 with perfect measurements with big, bow legs.

Legs that would get me into all kinds of trouble.

I wasn't a curser, probably because my parents didn't curse. So, I had the perfect image, I was a classy woman, some would say.

The truth was, I was far from classy. I was a lost, no class, slut fallen into the cracks of the low life. You can look good when you are comparing yourself to those that have fallen lower than yourself. Even you begin to believe the lie that you are all together, but you know what goes on behind closed doors.

Let's go back to the beginning of this awesome, life changing year, 1979! *I have marked some of the **Chess Moves** along the way.*

My New Year's Resolution
January 1, 1979 A.D.

No smoking! Did you really think I was going to say, no sex!?

At the end of every year, I would take a good hard look at my life. I realized that I was doing and feeling a little bit better about myself. Yes, I was a slut, but my bills were paid, even had a few dollars saved, and had begun to travel a little. I had even incorporated church twice a month into my routine.

Chess Move!

Being an analytical person, I concluded that my church attendance was making a difference in my life. So, my New Year's Resolution was to attend church every Sunday. The plan was to go out and party on Friday and stay in on Saturday to prepare for Sunday church.

Each week, I felt a change in me even though I was still living the low-life. Often, I found myself crying especially while in church. After having sex, I felt so dirty; it seemed that regardless of how hard I scrubbed and put cologne on, it wasn't working anymore.

Even the cigarettes were beginning to have a detestable smell. I was smoking almost two packs a day. I decided to make another attempt to stop smoking cigarettes. I had tried in 1978; I went seven months with my willpower. However, when I started back, I smoked more to seemingly catch-up.

Chess Move!

I decided to try another method since my willpower had failed. I had learned in church that I could call on the Name of Jesus and receive deliverance and victory in whatever area I needed. So, I tried calling on the Name of Jesus, whenever I had the urge to smoke a cigarette. I realized that I had to make up my mind that no one was forcing me with a gun to put a cigarette in my mouth. I told myself that regardless of how much my body craved nicotine, I was in control. I would call out loud, "Jesus, Jesus, Jesus" until the craving would go away. I must admit, it wasn't easy, it is a real addiction. The withdrawal wasn't as bad as it was when I made an attempt the previous year. I was munching a lot, and I noticed I was gaining weight from consistently putting food in my mouth instead of cigarettes.

A few weeks went by, one day I realized that I didn't binge eat nor have any cravings for cigarettes. I don't know the day or hour; it just was no longer an issue. I had gotten the Victory over Nicotine Addiction!!

Glory to God, I haven't smoked a cigarette since January 1979!!

There have been times that the urge has returned, especially if I am experience some challenging times. Death in the family or family situations, lack of money, personal relationship issues and the like. I just resort back to what I know works, I call on the Name of Jesus.

The devil will always challenge your victory; you can't ever forget the lessons learned.

Chess Move!

An old high school buddy reappeared into my life. Samuel was a lost soul too, who came from a wonderful, Christian family. He was struggling with addictions too but was ready for a new life. Even though we sinned 6 days a week, on Sunday he would go to church with me and my daughter, Precious. I met Samuel's family, and even though they didn't care for me and thought that he deserved better, I did get points because he had started to go back to church.

One Sunday, after attending church, Samuel wanted to take us to meet his saved sister and her husband, Judith and John who were ministers. Samuel was feeling good about himself and wanted to show us off. We were greeted warmly; even though we had arrived at dinner time. They just sat three more plates, and we sat around the dining table and had dinner with them and their two children, a boy and girl. I was shocked; I didn't realize that families used real china and ate together on days that weren't holidays. This looked like a scene from the Ozzie and Harriet TV show. What a great impression, the dad was actually having dinner with his family.

You are going to be surprised about what we talked about; I should say they because they did most of the talking. We intently listened as they shared one testimony after another of the goodness of GOD and the miracles that they were experiencing in their lives. The more that they talked, the more excited they became. Their faces seemed to radiate more and more. The husband and wife were talking at the same time, she would begin the story, and he would finish. Each story would remind them of another story. We sat at the table for what seemed like hours. I wasn't bored; I actually didn't want them to stop. I had never heard testimonies like these and how God was personally involved in their daily lives. The children were in their play area having a ball with Precious.

Chess Move!
The ministers calmed down and shifted gears. The husband invited Samuel in his study to continue talking, while we remained at the table.

Minister Judith quickly seized the opportunity to interrogate me. That is what big sisters do, right? I had let my guard down because the atmosphere in her home was so inviting and warm. I wasn't threatened by her interrogation. When she asked me about the type of church I attended, I must have given her the wrong answer because her facial expression went sour. Her voice became harsh, and she asked me why that particular church? I was surprised at her response; I thought she would be glad that at least I was attending a church and her brother was going with me. I humbled myself and responded that this was something new to me, and I have to start somewhere. She instantly saw my sincerity and backed off. Needless to say, it was time to make our departure.

But I did return later for a visit, by myself.

Every week I found myself looking forward to attending church. It was fun dressing up to go somewhere besides the nightclubs. I was learning so much. One day, as I was driving along, without thinking, I said, "I want to be saved." I thought, where did that come from?

My eyes seemed to be opening up for the first time; I saw things in a different light. The world looked so dirty and messed up. I had a yearning for order and cleanliness. I found myself being uncomfortable with my associates and their conversations. Their wretchedness seemed to be magnified. The cussing was repulsive and seemed so ignorant.

I was ready for something, but I didn't know what I was seeking. I thought, who can help me find my way? I came to a conclusion that I was now old enough to have some answers. That being silent on the topic of God wasn't good enough. Yes, it seemed that everyone had a different opinion of God. Someone had to be right, and somebody had to be wrong. So, I started my search. I began going to various churches and meetings. I ruled out nothing; if someone came across my path and they professed that they knew the Way to God, I would take them at their word. I would follow them to see if they had what I was searching for. I was disappointed time after time. They would be going to church or meetings just like I was but without any victory. They were still sleeping around, drinking, cussing, and living the same low life as me. I ran into all kinds of religious folk during this time of seeking.

Chess Move!
Women are often sidetracked by other women. Our defense guards are up, looking for the enemy to use a male, but he often uses women.

I met a young lady named Anne who seemed to have it together. I visited her church, and after several visits, I joined. They gave me a box of envelopes for my money offerings and explained my financial obligations to the church. After a few weeks, I began to feel burdened financially. It seemed as if I had taken on another bill. I certainly didn't feel the relief that I desired; the void was worse!

The more that I came to know Anne, I saw that her state of being was worse off than mine. She was living with a man who wasn't her husband. When I asked her about it, she said that they were married in the sight of God and that was all that mattered. She would tell me of episodes of outbursts of anger that she would have when she was displeased.

Yet, she was promoted in her church, and designated an Elect Lady and sat in the front pew of the church. Something is wrong here; didn't God tell the leadership that her life was not in order. I just thought that a person should be honorable to hold such a title. I had a lot to learn, right?

Chess Move!
Don't be deceived by the fact that a person attends church. Everyone is at a different season of their journey. The scriptures

state, "Let them alone. They are *blind* leaders of the *blind*. And if the *blind leads* the *blind*, both will fall into a ditch." Matthew 15:14

In retrospect, Anne was a leader. The question is who was she working for? She had every right to sit in the first pew because she was actively bringing new souls into the clutches of the enemy. I was one of them, but not for long!

Praise Break!
It was March, three months still NO cigarettes and I was going to church every Sunday!!

I decided to not go back to Anne's church. Throughout my journey, regardless of what was doing wrong and how far off that I was, I could always feel God's presence. Whenever I felt that I had ventured down the wrong road, I would always allow God to back me up to square one. The key is to take a breather, re-group in your mind, get back up and continue because you know that you will find your answer sooner or later.

The Search continues: Ok, now I'm back to square one, but I did remember to call on the Name of Jesus. When I did, He answered, Minister Judith, Samuel's sister came to mind. I decided to call and ask if I could visit her without her brother. She happily said, "Yes."

At the end of our lovely visit, Judith invited me to her church. I left her home with a sigh of relief; I knew I was on the right track. I purposed to attend her church that next Sunday.

Chess Move!

Sunday didn't come fast enough. My daughter and I ventured alone since Samuel had moved on, and no longer called or visited us. As I look back, I realized that he was used to connect me with his sister. I will never forget my experience at this church. It was so different from the dark places that I had been attending. The atmosphere was so pleasing and peaceful. At the end of the worship service, I went to the altar for prayer. One of the young lady ministers kneeled in front of me and prayed fervently for me. I felt so peaceful and believed that God was really hearing her prayers. All of a sudden, I smelled this foul, disgusting smell. Where is that coming from? I realized that I had a discharge from my body. I was so embarrassed because I knew that the prayer warrior smelled it too.

As we were walking out of the church, it felt as if whatever was happening to me stopped and that I had to return to that church for God to continue the process. I found out that they were meeting again that evening at 6 pm. I had never gone to church twice on a Sunday, but we had to go back.

My hanging buddies were waiting for me to come home from church to get high. When I told them no and that I was going back to church that evening, they actually didn't believe me. I couldn't blame them; I didn't believe it.

That evening was marvelous, it was so different from anything that I had ever experienced. The Christians were so loving and welcoming to us. We felt like they were our family. When service was over, as I walked through the door to leave, I had the same thought that I had to come back for more. I discovered that they had Bible Study on Wednesday at 7 pm.

Well, you know where I was on Wednesday! I had broken another record, attending church three times in one week. I anxiously anticipated attending Bible Study. Perhaps, I would finally get an understanding of the Bible. I would get so frustrated when reading the Bible, it seemed like a foreign language or that it was written in a code.

Now, my daughter enjoyed church as well, but three times in one week was a bit much for her. We had to have a discussion on the way to church, and I had to remind her who was the mother. She put on a smile, but she wasn't happy with our new agenda.

Wow, Awesome, and Very Informative would be the words to describe Wednesday Bible Study. I realized how ignorant I was of God's Word. I always had a Bible, but seldom used it because I didn't understand it. So, this is the reason people attend Bible Study in the middle of the week, to actually learn what's in the Bible. Duh! I really felt stupid, not being able to turn to the scriptures. My daughter was looking at me fumbling through the pages of the Bible as if she was embarrassed. I determined that by next Wednesday, I would have a new notebook just for church notes. I felt challenged, after all, I was an A student all throughout my school years. I just had gotten off track, but this new awakening to learn is feeling good. At the conclusion of class, as we walked out of the doors of the church, the process came to a halt. Ok, I get this, Friday was the next meeting at 7 pm.

Chapter 2
Checkmate

Crossover Friday
March 13, 1979 A.D.

The memory is still fresh in my mind: I gave my daughter a break from church. I had gotten someone to watch her for the night. I would pick her up in the morning; I had business to take care of, but I stopped by the church.

FRIDAY CHURCH!!
These people are really strange, church almost every day! Wow, I can't believe that I'm going to church on a Friday night. They say that the eagle flies on Friday, it's payday for most folk. So, you know I need to be out taking care of business, but I feel a need to stop by the church to get another touch. I'm sounding like an addict; I need to stop by the church to get a fix.

I must admit, something is happening to me, and it feels really good. I'm calm, not nervous, or having a sense of fear that something bad is getting ready to happen. I am not worried about anything; I really believe that God is leading me and will take care of us.

Being a single parent; well, actually I am married, but he doesn't help with our daughter. My first husband, my daughter's dad lives in another state and never sends money. When he comes to town, he may take our daughter shopping and buys whatever she wants but not what she needs.

I desire to be a great parent like my mom and dad were. I don't see how they did it with 5 children. My dad was the sole breadwinner; he didn't want mother to work.

Ok, I talked myself into breaking another record, FRIDAY CHURCH!! My friends and family are wondering if I've lost it and am joining a cult.

This Was My Plan!
I told my guy, who pays me to have sex with him that I would be over at 9 pm. I was going to drop by the church just to see what they do on Friday when everyone else is out having fun.

I sat at the back of the church. I really felt like a spy and totally out of place especially with pants on. I hoped no one would really notice that I was breaking the No Pants rule and they were really tight. I had worn all my decent looking skirts and dress earlier in the week. I will just stay in the back and slip out unnoticed before church ends.

The singing was very lively; I was beginning to learn some of the words. I found myself singing them at home. My daughter was singing different songs too.

Then it happened!!

They stopped singing, and a full-figured woman wearing a long black skirt took the microphone. Honestly, she didn't need a mic, her voice was as big as she was. I can't tell you what she was saying, but her words were piercing me. I started to squirm in my seat. I really needed to make my exit; it was time to go. Maybe this is a cult; I never experienced this before.

I couldn't move my feet, I was beginning to feel like a prisoner. It would help if she shut up with all that loud talking. I haven't seen her before, she must be the Friday Night Special Guest Speaker. This is what I get for being noisy; church four times in a week was too much.

Then she lowered the volume of her voice to a whisper. It made me want to hear her conclusion, but then she hooked me. I felt like a fish that had grabbed the bait; she asked if anyone who wanted prayer to come to the front. I felt a tug, an urge to go to the altar, but I had pants on, and besides, I have this man with a pocket full of money waiting for me.

The struggle was on, I was determined not to go up there, but I couldn't turn my feet to walk out to the safety of my car. She was so patient, her eyes seemed to be on me with a look of determination to catch me. It was like a tug of war where there is a line in the sand, and opposing teams are holding different ends of a rope. The object of the game is to be the strongest and pull the opposing person or team across the line in the middle.

I Crossed Over Without Realizing It!
Honestly, I don't remember walking up there. All the ministers converged and surrounded me. Oddly enough, it was peaceful there. The atmosphere really did feel different than sitting in the back.

I stopped fighting, relaxed, and closed my eyes. I could hear them praying and the music but I was in another place. It felt as if I was floating without a care in the world. I was totally into this place that I had never experienced before. No worries, my daughter wasn't even on my mind, nothing!

The pastor, an elderly, short stout woman, asked me if I wanted to be saved? I nodded my head. She asked me if I believed that Jesus died for me on the cross. I thought, I wasn't there but if it is in the Bible, then I believe, I said yes.

Then, I began to have Flashbacks, one after another. It was like a movie of my past life! It was the times and places that were buried inside of me. It was the scenes that I didn't talk about and tried to not think about.

I began to cry when I saw the room and the shadow of the man that was on top of me, reciting poetry or scriptures as he raped me. He was so strong; I struggled, but he had me pinned down. I was hopeless, in exhaustion, I surrendered. As he enjoyed himself, my next thought was the concern for my life and how I was going to escape from the crazy man.

Then another Flashback: the police pulled me over for not stopping at a Stop sign. It was night and the flashing lights and the bullhorn demanding that I stop almost gave me a heart attack. Especially because I was transporting a delivery of marijuana and pills to sell.

Then another Flashback: I was arguing with a lover, and he began to choke me, I actually saw stars as I was gasping for air. I almost died that night.

All of a sudden, I realized that God had been with me in each situation!! It was because of Him that I am alive. I always thought it was because I was lucky or just smart enough to maneuver out of the many close calls with death.

I began to cry out from the depth of my soul, "Thank You, Jesus!" over and over until the words no longer would come out of my mouth. My mouth was moving but no sound.

Checkmate! GOD Wins!
At that point, the Pastor knew actually what move to make! She gently laid her hands on my throat and told me to relax. All of a sudden, my mouth began to quiver, and this beautiful song in an unfamiliar language came out of my mouth. Was

that beautiful melody coming from me? The more that I sang, the better that I felt. It was so supernatural, I didn't question if it was God or the devil. It had to be God because it was so soothing to my soul. I could have gone on forever, but I was interrupted when they tapped me on my shoulders. I opened my eyes, and the church was no longer full, lights were dimmed, and the few remaining were ready to go home. They jokingly told me that I could stop speaking in tongues and start again whenever I wanted. They explained that I had gotten saved and was filled with the Holy Spirit with the evidence of speaking in tongues. What were they talking about? I had never heard that term, and was clueless to what had taken place on the *Friday evening, March 13, 1979.*

Chapter 3
Learning to Live the Good Life
The Process

Picking Up the Pieces

God's ways and thoughts are certainly not our ways and thoughts. When I say it was Checkmate, Game Over, I truly mean it. God's Hand came down and knocked Satan over and lifted me out of darkness. He took full control of my life.

It was just that drastic, a totally different lifestyle from that evening on. A new life that I would have to learn how to live. I was 27 years old, but I was still a babe born into a new way of life. As a natural baby desires natural milk, I also craved the milk of God's Word. I couldn't get enough of the scriptures. The Holy Spirit was giving me understanding of the Word. I would study my notes after each Bible class or church service. I wanted to make sure that what I was being taught was the truth. I didn't miss a service; whenever the doors opened, I was there. My daughter certainly wasn't happy about this. Nor my associates, especially the paying kind. One of the men had the nerves to say that I had reneged on our arrangement. Another said that I would be back because of my love for money.

My family had various opinions on my change. Many were happy for me but didn't think it would last. I went back to each associate and personally told them of my experience and invited them to join me. No one took me up on my offer. Eventually, we parted ways. It was painful and lonesome at times. Sitting at home reading my Bible every day was sometimes boring. Occasionally, I would get invited out, but I said no. I was wise enough to know that there was no turning back. I was over that life.

GOD in His Wisdom knew that I needed to be isolated and protected during this vulnerable baby-stage of my Christian life. He told me to quit my job. I worked in our family business and had a key role in the daily activities. Many of those associates that I had to distance myself from were still able to have contact with me because we served the public. GOD pulled me out, just like that. He hid me for months, some I never saw again.

My income was drastically reduced; I had to return my new sports car, and start to ride the bus. It was a rude awakening for both my daughter and myself. I had to learn to budget-shop for our needs. I learned how to shop at resale stores and use coupons. Today, I am truly grateful for my experience because it taught us survival skills and how to be grateful for the little as well as much.

Looking Back to Move Forward
Chess Move!

Year 1979 to 1982, God put me in isolation for the first three years of my new life. No job, no dating, basically church and back home. I didn't have much interaction with family because we had become so incompatible. My presence made them uncomfortable, so I spared them by not coming around.

I was always bothered by two things. One, I had really disappointed my dad because I dropped out of college due to being pregnant. And the other was the guilt and the sense of loss because of an abortion.

I was the eldest child, an honor student. During my high school senior year, classmates had nominated me Most Likely to Succeed. I had received a full scholarship to the University of Detroit. I was on my way to becoming a lawyer, but I got pregnant during my first year. My dad was so hurt and would often remind me of how disappointed he was. I wanted to make my dad proud. I believe that before he passed away, he was proud of my accomplishments.

God brought comfort to me when he told me to get a degree in His Word. As I said, I would take notes at every church function. I didn't just take notes, but I diligently studied them and researched the scriptures. I remember when I graduated to the Master Level in the spirit realm. Yes, I have a Doctorate Degree in the Word of God, given to me by my Father who is in heaven. This revelation has given me peace in regards to my education. I have since gone to two Bible colleges and have been certified and ordained as a minister.

I know many educated people that have graduated from well-known secular universities but do not know the books of the Bible. They may recall Bible stories that they learned as a child. When a crisis occurs, they are spiritually weak because of the lack of the knowledge of God's Word. I will discuss later the importance of having God's Word in you during a battle.

Now, the second thing of my past that haunted me was that I had an abortion once I was married. I had earlier contemplated an abortion when I was pregnant with my daughter, thank God, I didn't, she is my only living child that I birthed. My parents had encouraged me to get the abortion and continue my education. We made the appointment, dad dropped mother and me off at the doctor for an illegal procedure. I gave them $300 and undressed, got on the table. When the doctor inserted the first instrument, I couldn't bear the pain. The doctor said very bluntly, "You weren't so sensitive when you were getting pregnant." That was all that I needed; I told him to stop and got off the table. When my dad picked us up, and my Mother told him the seemingly bad news, he was very upset. When we got home, he dropped us off in the alley behind our house. He told me that if I had anything to say to him to relay it to my mother. Well, that didn't help my relationship with my dad. I was a daddy's girl, I loved my dad dearly, but I seemed to be digging a deeper hole for myself.

So, my parents came up with Plan B; I needed to get married! What! I had already made one mistake, I knew that getting married would be another. The only positive that I saw was that I would be able to get out of their home and start my adult life.

I graduated in February, pregnant and married by October same year, 1969. I was the hot gossip news among my family and classmates. It was hard to hold my head up during those days.

I felt so alone sitting in our studio apartment. We got married on a Friday at City Hall witnessed by my mother and his dad. I remember, his dad said that he would not marry his son even if he was pregnant with triplets. Nonetheless, I knowingly made the wrong decision out of honor to my parents and wanting to be "grown." After the short marriage ceremony, my teenage husband and I went to our cute studio apartment and consummated our marriage. Later that evening, he proceeded to dress to go out. When I asked him where he was going, he said to a gambling party. He asked me if I wanted to go, of course, I said no. I had never gone to such a party, I was the good girl that was attracted to the bad, fast type of guy.

He said ok, and took all of our money which we had for furniture being delivered C.O.D. the next day. As soon as, he closed the door, I began to cry because I knew that I had made a terrible mistake. Well, to my surprise, within a couple of minutes, he burst through the door and announced that he remembered that I was his wife, and from that day forward I was to do whatever he said, and he wanted me to be with him. I felt so out of place; a woman told me that I didn't need to be there. Well, needless to stay, he lost all of our money. This was our first day as husband and wife.

The pregnancy was very difficult, probably because of the stress. It was a terrible marriage, by our third month of marriage, seven months pregnant, I was back home living with my parents. I vomited every meal every day for the entire nine months. I only gained 8 pounds; the doctor told me to just make sure I took my vitamin every day. My dad took me to the hospital during the middle of the night when I went into labor. He had just taken me shopping for some maternity clothes; he had forgiven me. My baby weighed 7 pounds and 13 ounces to everyone's surprise. She was healthy and beautiful. Something good did come out of all my pain and disappointment.

Her dad went off to the army and I was left to raise our baby. He had planned for us to get together once he finished basic training. Well, by the time of our planned reunion and my move to the army base, I had gotten an appetite for the nightlife. I guess, he too had second thoughts about me coming there. So, I moved with a girlfriend, and the party was on. I quickly learned that men would tell you what you want to hear to get what they want. However, I was slow to learn how to deal with them without getting emotionally involved. All of my girlfriends were in the same boat. We would have pity parties all the time. The challenge was who could tell the saddest story.

I found out a lot about myself during that time; I am a giving and very compassionate person. Many people especially men would take my kindness for a weakness. I was slow at adjusting to the world's way of "I will get you before you get me." I began to wear a necklace with the word Bitch in bold letters. My mother absolutely despised my wearing such a demeaning piece of jewelry. I was making a statement to the world that I wanted to be hardcore even though I wasn't at all.

Once my baby's daddy got out of the army, we decided to move together. I didn't count the cost because he still lived as a single person, and so did I. It was crazy and a very stressful life. We would separate and get back together time and time again. At one point, I determined that I needed to stop running. It lasted six months, this time I was forced to leave because of a nervous breakdown. I couldn't take the crazy lifestyle anymore, and my nerves just shut down.

Proverbs 13:15 says, *"The way of a transgressor is hard."* I was so out of the Will of God that He had to bring me to my knees. The day of the breakdown, I left our home as usual. I got to work, I was training for a new position which added to my stress. My head began to ache, then it got worse and worse. I couldn't hold my head up. I was taken to the hospital from work. I was there for a few days. My grandmother was ill and was in the same hospital. Every day, I would visit her room and sit with her. She was unable to speak but would just stare at me. I believe that she was praying for me. Lord knows, I needed it.

I went to live with my mom and dad. They nursed me back to health again. When I got well, I was back to hanging out in the streets. My dad eventually put me out because I was staying out all night; mind you, I was still legally married.

My health began to fail again; this time I was diagnosed with an overactive thyroid. I looked terrible; my eyes were bulging out of my head, my complexion was an ashy gray, and I had lost a lot of weight. I felt terrible, my heart was always racing. The doctors said my metabolism was going seven times too fast. My family thought I was on drugs, no one came to ask me. I didn't know what was going on with me and I didn't have the wisdom to go to the doctor sooner.

One day, I went to the dentist to have a tooth extracted. While there, I picked up a magazine and read an article about the most wrongly diagnosed ailment: hyperthyroidism. It described the symptoms; sometimes you feel like just going outside and screaming at the top of your lungs. That was me. I went to a doctor, and my diagnosis were correct. I had a goiter in my neck which caused all the above symptoms. I had a choice between surgery and a dose of the atomic capsule, radioactive iodine. I feared surgery so I chose the other.

The day that I took the radioactive iodine I had to go into isolation to not affect anyone. They had explained that the dosage amount was purely guesswork and hoped that it wouldn't remove too much of the thyroid. Well, it did, and now I have been diagnosed with hypothyroidism. I take an iodine supplement every day to balance my system.

At one point, I was on 24 pills a day. I couldn't function because I was in a drugged state. I would wake up by an alarm clock to take my daughter to school, return home, take another dose and sleep until time to pick her up. Precious literally took care of us during this time. She was seven years old.

I would smoke marijuana on the days that I needed to stay awake to go to the doctor for more prescribed drugs. Needless to stay, I was a walking zombie. I honestly didn't realize that I was a drug addict because they were legally prescribed to me.

Chess Move!
Pistol Packing Bettie
I met the majority of the bad guys while on my job. I worked at my family business; a car wash, music & electronics store. Guys loved to stop by to get their cars hand washed and buy the latest music and gadgets. I was trained to smile and cater to them.

Charles was a very sweet guy. Yes, he was a thug with a criminal record, but had a big heart. He had compassion for me, a single mother. He was always looking out for me.

I was shocked when he proudly presented me with a gun. He said that I needed a gun for protection since I lived alone. He showed me how to use it. I was never comfortable with the gun in my house because of Precious being so curious.

I believe that him giving me the gun was a set up. I was always fearful of my daughter playing with the gun and having an accident.

Many times, I contemplated grabbing the gun in a fit of anger. I was glad when the gun was confiscated. God blocked the enemy's plan!

Chess Move!
I mentioned earlier that I had experienced being raped. One day in my zombie state, I was out shopping for a smaller, less expensive apartment because I was behind on my rent. I was dressed very inappropriately for daytime business. I'm not making excuses for the rapist, but my attire encouraged him by giving the impression that I was for hire. The manager took me around the building to show the vacant apartments. There was one that I really liked. The last one that he took me to was furnished. When we entered that apartment, I sensed that this was his home. He asked me to sit down and proceeded to make casual conversation. I attempted to keep the conversation on a business level by telling him which apartment I wanted. I counted out the money and laid it on the table. He continued to talk about other things. So again, to keep it business, I asked him for a receipt. He wrote out the receipt but didn't give it to me. He left it in the receipt book.

Then he asked me the question that would always get my attention. "Do you believe in God?" I said, Yes. He then got up and told me to follow him, that he wanted to show me something. In hindsight, as I am writing, I should have run at that point. But no, I followed him into the next room which I found was empty except for a small, low table. He pointed to a picture frame, when I bent down to read, I saw that it was a

Bible verse. At that p oint, I realized that I was in trouble. He was standing behind me, when I straightened up, he attacked me and threw me on the floor. We wrestled until I was exhausted and he had penned my arms and legs down. All the time, he was quoting bible verses. I had often thought that no man could actually rape a woman, that she just surrendered and gave in. I personally know that is not true, this man overpowered me and violated my rights and forced me to allow him to use my body for his pleasure.

After the sexual act was over, he came to himself and started laughing. He blamed me and said that I had distracted him from his work. He told me to go to the other bathroom to clean up while he went into the master bath. He continued to sing as he went to clean up. In the meantime, I didn't stop, I went straight to the front door, but then I noticed my money and the receipt. I tore the receipt out of the book, grabbed my money, and took off running. I didn't wait for the elevators; I ran down at least seven flights of stairs. When I got to the lobby, I calmed down and walked out of the building.

When I got to the car, my adrenaline was racing. I sat there for a moment, I realized that I wasn't physically hurt. I looked at the money and the receipt and began to laugh. You see, I always associated being emotionally involved with having sex. I often said that I couldn't have sex for money. But here I was with a new revelation, that it wasn't that bad and I could do it. That was the beginning of my career of prostitution. Mind you that I was an entrepreneur at heart. So, I considered this as a business. On that day, I lost something very precious. I became very bitter and ruthless. An associate of mine took the receipt to the apartment a few days later, and they refunded my money. There was a new manager; the rapist had gotten fired. We laughed and got high with the money.

Chess Move!
At that point, my life began its downward spiral. I had a false sense of freedom. I was still on the drugs and using marijuana to function. I would sleep all day and hit the streets at night. I had a nice, cute, air conditioned apartment that was perfect for my daughter and me. I had a nice vehicle and had the appearance of a single mom taking care of business.

Every night, I went out looking for trouble. When I look back at my life, I could stop right now and cry. It is the grace of God that I survived to be able to tell you my story. One night, I was going from one joint to the next; I always traveled alone because I was ashamed of my night lifestyle. I was driving along when I realized that I was lost, not because of an unfamiliar location but lost because I didn't know where I was going. I pulled over and asked myself what my destination was. You know you may get up to go to the next room and forget what you wanted. Same thing, but this was in the middle of the night.

Chess Move!
Ok, that was a wakeup call... I realized that I was losing it. I decided to stop getting high. I realized that every time that I smoked marijuana that I would have a different reaction. So, in

all actuality, I didn't know what I was smoking. I stopped smoking marijuana, my supplier was very disappointed. Next, the pills had to go, this is when I realized that I was addicted. One day, I was having severe withdrawal, and I found myself tearing up my closet to get them. I stopped and looked at myself in the mirror and determined that I was going to have to do this cold turkey.

I stayed in for months, I had a small plant in the window that I watched grow. I literally would look at this plant all throughout the day to see if it grew. That plant gave me life as I watched it slowly grow and begin to get stronger and stronger.

But the devil wasn't through with me. Now I am drug-free and my mind is stable. I am no longer walking the streets for money. I had decided it was time to do business a little differently. I made several business arrangements for my services on a weekly basis. Appointments only. I was truly deceived, I referred to these men as my Sugar Daddies. I pray that as I am being transparent with you that your eyes will open to your upside-down lifestyle. I really thought that I had it going on; I had money sufficient to take care of us and a healthy bank account.

Chess Move!
All was well until a ghost of my past showed up. The one that I was always weak for. He had moved out of town, but I heard that he had resurfaced and was trying to find me. Just knowing that he was close, made me crave him. So, I made the same

mistake that I had made so many times before, I let him back into our lives.

When he came over to visit, he instantly took over, moving furniture and complaining about this and that. He asked for a key; everything within me was crying No. But I was weak and gave in and got a key made for him.

It was lovely for a while; we had planned to move into a larger place. So we agreed to open a bank account together and to make a deposit each week. I went into my savings and matched what he was putting in. Both of our names were on the account. Things were going along as planned. But I didn't like his lack of visits and attention. I began to feel like a prisoner because I wasn't accustomed to being accountable to anyone.

One night, out of boredom, I dressed and went out on the town. I partied until early in the morning. When he called and asked how I spent last night, I lied and said I was home. I didn't know that he had come by. He came right over, and we argued. When he calmed down and fell asleep, I took my door keys off his key ring.

A couple of hours later, he got up to leave. I was so relieved when he closed the door. But he had forgotten his cell phone and realized that I had taken my keys back when he tried to open the door.

He was so angry that he kicked my door down when I wouldn't let him in. He threw me on the floor and began choking me. I was gasping for air, as I began to lose consciousness, an idea came to me to pretend that I was already dead. He left me lying there for dead.

It took me a couple of days to recover and get the house secured. I decided to check our bank account; you guessed it. It was all gone, every penny. Stupid, stupid, stupid.

I was down but not out. I decided to move to another place and make a new start. This time, I moved into an upper flat, it was very nice. I decorated it and made it very comfortable and suitable to entertain my paying guests. Business as usual, my goal was to replenish my bank account and do some traveling.

I was working at our family business and making money as a prostitute on the side. I thought I had figured out the system. I was sure that just working a job wasn't going to get me the wealth I desired. I did the only thing I knew and used the resource that I had, my body.

One day, one of my clients said that he had taken his wife on a vacation to Hawaii. I began to realize that what he gave me was his spare change; it didn't affect his home life. I was just a plaything on the side, so he wasn't giving up anything. I was giving more because I was giving of myself. I began to feel the old Bettie surface. The woman that desired to vacation with a husband, to have a loving relationship and build a home for my daughter.

Praise Break!
An occasional look back has helped me to continue on.

I was also informed on that unforgettable Friday, that when I accepted Jesus that the Blood that He shed on the cross, washed my sins away.

Thank God, for the Blood that continues to wash me.

"But if we walk in the light as He is in the light, we have fellowship with one another, and the blood of Jesus Christ His Son cleanses us from all sin." 1 John 1:7

Chapter 4
School of Wisdom
Crash Course, Take Copious Notes

Chess Move!
I decided to attend every service at church. I was determined to live this new life. It was very hard to change completely. Even after getting saved, there were days when the money was low, and I've gone to pick up the phone and call one of my sugar daddies. I would hang up the phone and cry out for God's help because I didn't know how to live by faith. All I knew was how to make up the shortage by using my body.

One Sunday at church, I went to the altar for prayer. I was so burdened because I was behind on my rent. I had taken my rent money and bought my daughter's gifts for Christmas. I had taken her shopping at the dollar store. It wasn't much, but it made her happy.

God spoke to my heart to stop trying to be her mother and father, but for me to continue to be a good mother and He would be the Father. It was a deal; I left the altar with a sigh of relief. From that day to this one, I do not worry about my daughter. God has been faithful to meet her every need and some of her wants.

The landlord's demands no longer frightened me or had me hiding from him. I began to face my creditors and every other issue head-on. My new philosophy was to take the bull by the horn. I started to learn the scriptures, one was Psalms 118:6 *"The LORD is on my side, I will not fear: what can man do to me?"* and another was, *"So we may boldly say: 'The LORD is my helper, and I will not fear what man shall do unto me.'"* Hebrews 13:6. I eventually caught up with my rent and my landlord and I began to have a good relationship of mutual respect.

Life as a born-again Christian is very different from the worldly life that I had lived for 27 years. It was like starting off in nursery school. A whole new world. The Bible has all the rules and directions that I need. I was hungry for this new knowledge and understanding. I had made so many mistakes, and each one cost me time, money or dignity. I wanted to recover what I had lost, and limiting or eliminating mistakes was vital.

It seemed that my eyesight was 20/20, I could see clearly now. Stuff that the enemy was able to pull over my eyes, no longer worked. My hearing was more sensitive, hearing curse words irritated my ears. I could no longer watch violent movies.

I quickly learned that the Holy Spirit was present to clean up my life in every area.

Liars Go to Hell!
"A false witness will not go unpunished, and he who speaks lies shall perish." Proverbs 19:9

The Holy Spirit didn't have a problem with convicting me every time I told a lie. I thought it was just exaggeration, that's all. I realized that I lied every day without reason. It is just what sinners do.

Repentance became my pastime. I was quick to repent when the Holy Spirit told me that I was sinning. I would just feel so awful after I had lied or done something that was not pleasing to God. It was just not worth it.

At the end of each day, I would check to see where I had missed it. Most times, it would be something that I was unaware of. It was just my former nature to sin. Well, thank God that we have the opportunity to get it right. Repentance, the act of asking for forgiveness and turning from the sin, is wonderful. It is not true repentance if we ask for forgiveness and do it again because we know the blood of Jesus washes us. No, this is not a game. I was sincere, and each day my ways became more like the God that I was now serving.

Sinners do what sinners do. With that understanding, I handle those that are still walking in darkness with a long-handled spoon.

Complete Wardrobe Change!

*"Don't be concerned about the outward beauty of fancy hairstyles, expensive jewelry, or beautiful clothes. 4 You should clothe yourselves instead with the beauty that comes from within, the unfading beauty of a gentle and quiet spirit, which is so precious to God. "*1 Peter 3:3-4 New Living Translation

I didn't know how to dress appropriately. I had learned to dress seductively. I thought that my finest trait was my legs, so I wore short skirts and dresses most of the time. All of that had to be thrown away; I no longer felt comfortable in them. I had to pray for God to show me how to dress conducive to my new identity. The authentic Bettie was being released. I no longer looked at magazines or others for fashion ideas.

Chess Move

Nor did I look at the women at church because some came dressed to seduce. So, I decided to start from scratch and just took off all my makeup and wore long skirts and became a plain Jane. Over the years, we have refined my authentic look. I dress the way that I feel. I started wearing facial makeup and eyeshadow, until one day, God said that I was covering up His Glory, so I stopped. It's all natural, what you see is what you get.

I always get compliments on my skin; many say I have a glow. It's Jesus!!

As I look at the styles of today, I notice that women wear a lot of artificial, synthetic everything. Hair, nails, eyes, breast, and other body parts, lashes, I'm sure I'm missing something. The long, straight hair is truly a trend with my young sisters, to look like the popular singer that we all love.

It is so liberating to look into the mirror and see the image of Bettie, without the fixings. As I looked at the scripture, I saw that God addresses our attire. He doesn't miss anything. He looks beyond all the make-up and fixings to see what is in your heart. You can't cover it up, no matter how you try.

You Still Have to Reap What You Sow!
Living the Word of God will bring great results. During the years, 1979-1982, I still struggled, but I had peace and joy and didn't complain. I quickly understood that some of my discomforts were because of the past decisions I had made. *"Do not be deceived, God is not mocked; for whatever a man sows, that he will also reap."* Galatians 6:7 So I understand that the fruit of those bad seeds that I sowed living the life of a Bad Girl would soon be in my past. I determined to sow only good seeds as I lived the life of a Good Girl. I knew that one day, the good would catch up and run me over!!

"And all these blessings shall come upon you and overtake you because you obey the voice of the LORD your God." Deuteronomy 28:2

New Associates! Learning What NOT TO Say!
I realized that I had to change my associates and my environment to live this new life. I tried to mix the two but

realized that I wasn't strong enough to go to certain places and entertain certain people. The darkness would overcome the little light that I had.

I was invited to my first Christian Fellowship at one of the saint's home.

It was so different, the lights were on, adults played board games, and of course, the music was unfamiliar to me. I felt so out of place. The ladies were in the kitchen cooking a meal fit for a king. I tried to make conversation by saying, "You all are cooking up a storm.'" I was quickly told that I had made a negative confession. Before the evening was over, I had mistakenly put my foot in my mouth several times. Each time, I was lovingly corrected.

On the way home, I told God that I didn't want to go around those critical kinds of people. He told me that they were good for me. I had to learn to speak life and death every day. Therefore, I began to be very quiet because I didn't want to say the wrong thing. It can be something like, "He makes me sick." or "He is driving me crazy." Here is another one, "I am so broke." The scriptures say, *"That life and death is in the power of your tongue..."* Proverbs 18:21.

I grew to love these saints; we got together often. They had the Gift of Hospitality down to a science. We would have good clean fun with no cursing or arguments. They love, love, love to cook and eat. They prided themselves on their specialty dishes. The men cooked just as well as the women.

As a result of fellowshipping with my first church family, I learned the basic, elementary, foundational principles, and doctrines from them. I will always be grateful to them.

Learning What TO Say! Creating with My Words!
"…God, who gives life to the dead and calls those things which do not exist as though they did." Romans 4:17

As I was learning what not to say, I was also learning that I can create the life I desired by speaking positively. This was really a challenge; it was as if I had to learn how to talk like a baby. The Bible says, *"To be slow to speak…"* James 1:19 which takes discipline. I began to speak my dreams out loud; my faith would increase as I heard the words that I dared to say. I described my new home, car, family, etc.

We are created in God's image, just as God spoke, *"Let there be light,"* and there was light. We have the same ability. When we aren't feeling our best, instead of confessing that I am sick, I rather say, "I thank God for my healing! I will get stronger and stronger each day." I have made that confession, even during the times that I felt my worst. The next hour, I would notice a change, each day feeling better and evidently with no symptoms at all.

Calling those things which be not, works for every circumstance in your life.

This is my daily confession!
I am a healthy, wealthy, and wise woman of God.
I am a happy, holy, humble, and meek woman of God.
I am a faithful and thankful woman of God.
I am beautiful inside and out.
I am blessed by the Best.
In Jesus' Name.

I Got a New Job!
I was the usher at the front door of the church! I was the first person that you would see. I wore a light blue blouse and dark skirt every single Sunday. I really didn't mind because it was cost-effective. One day, one of the sisters told me that she really had experienced a rough morning. She had struggled to get to church but when she saw my smile, her burden lifted. I took my job as the front door usher very seriously. It really makes a difference how people are greeted and treated in the House of God.

In Times of Trouble, Call on the Name of Jesus!
Call on the Name of Jesus

MOTHER! Was the first name I called on when in trouble. No one told me to do so; it was just automatic. She was the first person that I knew; she carried me in her womb for nine months. She did care for me; fed, bathe, and clothe me since I was born.

I knew that if I cried out her name, she would come running to my rescue.

I don't know when Jesus' Name began to take the place of my Mother's. When you think about it, mothers can only do so much, but Jesus is limitless. He is Ever Present, All Powerful and All Knowing!

He knows what you need even before you call, how good is that? The Bible says, *"It shall come to pass that before they call, I will answer; and while they are still speaking, I will hear."* Isaiah 65:24

I told you that I was delivered from nicotine and smoking cigarettes by calling on the Name of Jesus. I have a couple more testimonies regarding the Power of Jesus' Name. It behooves you to get His Name in your mouth!

One evening, my daughter and I were riding our bikes. We usually didn't ride after dark, so we were making haste getting back home. As we were passing a dark alley, a man on a motorcycle forced us into the alley. My daughter frightenedly looked at me, as if to call on me to get us out of the situation. I called out the Name of Jesus without thinking; it was automatic. The man raised the visor of his helmet, and shouted over the noise of the motorcycle, "What did you say?" I felt a boldness rise in me, and I again shouted even louder, "JESUS," loud and clear.

The man immediately turned around and sped away. I will never forget how calling on Jesus stopped that man in his tracks.

Another time, early one Sunday morning, Precious and I were walking to the bus stop to go to church. A seemingly vicious dog started running towards us. Again, I called on the Name of Jesus, and the dog, honestly stopped in his tracks and turned around and ran in the opposite direction. What a relief, I think I was more afraid of the dog than the motorcycle man!!

Remember, *"That whoever calls on the name of the LORD shall be saved."* Joel 2:32

Chapter 5
School of Experience
Show Them What You Are Made Out Of!

New Husband, New Life! 1983 A.D.
I never missed a Sunday; I was faithful to serve until I married and joined my husband's church. When it was time to move on, the church gave me a beautiful bridal shower. The wedding and reception were there; my pastor married us on a Friday evening by candlelight. The members were happy for me but hated to see me leave. I didn't return to visit for many years, when God closed that door, it was closed. I was prepared and ready to enter into a new life, and I couldn't look back.

My new life brought new doors of opportunity. I always wondered why I existed and what was my purpose. With each new assignment, I found that I had hidden talents and gifts that I wasn't using. Some were dormant because there was no reason to use them. I found that I was good at a lot of different things. Usually, whatever I attempted to do, I was above average on the task.

Along with this discovery, ego and pride wanted to puff up and take the credit. So, I began to fail at some projects, which caused me to experience some embarrassing moments but I learned a lifelong lesson.

"Pride goes before destruction, and a haughty spirit before a fall." Proverbs 16:18

God will share His Glory with no one. I realize that *"I can do absolutely nothing without Him."* John 15:5 but *"I can do all things through Christ who gives me strength."* Philippians 4:13

Let's Take a Praise Break, right here!!!!

New Church Family
My husband's church, was very different. It was huge, and there were a lot of people. My new husband knew a lot of people and would have different conversations when church dismissed. I would stand to the side and wait patiently for him. One day, this scripture came to my mind, *"A man who has friends must himself be friendly…"* Proverbs 18:24

The plan was to boldly go up to someone each church service and introduce myself. I made it a point to show that I was friendly. It worked, so after a while, my new husband had to wait until I was finished talking. God's Word works in all areas.

We didn't have a car, so we would catch two buses to church. Every Sunday, Wednesday, and Friday. Many times, the saints would blow their horns as they drove past us at the bus stop. I don't recall ever getting a ride home. My husband and I made a promise to God that when we got transportation, we would offer people rides to and from church. We always had a car full.

Do You Fear the Lord?
"Fear of the LORD is the foundation of wisdom. Knowledge of the Holy One results in good judgment." Proverbs 9:10

My dad made sure that all of his children feared him. He made certain that we understood his rules and consequences for disobedience, which only made me a good liar and schemer. I still did what I wanted, but I would sneak behind his back. When I got caught, I would face the punishment. I got away with more than my Dad could ever imagine.

As I reflect back on my childhood, teens, and young adult years, if I had the fear of the Lord, I would have made different decisions. I actually thought that because my father didn't catch me, that I had gotten away with my actions. When I would sneak off to do whatever Bettie wanted; I didn't realize that God was watching and He wasn't pleased.

Some months, my monthly cycle would be late. I would beg God to give me another chance not to be pregnant. When everything got back to normal, I would sneak off again until I got pregnant. It is so true that what you do in the dark will come to the light. *"For there is nothing covered that will not be revealed, nor hidden that will not be known."* Luke 12:2. Now, it was no longer a secret; everyone knew that quiet, studious, seemingly innocent Bettie wasn't so innocent.

The ungodly state of our world is due to the lack of the fear of the Lord. Most adults do not fear the Lord, therefore fail to impart to their children and grandchildren this trait. Thus, we have generations of lawlessness. Imagine how different the world would be if even 75% of the population feared God.

My dad was the best father that he knew how to be. I appreciate all of his efforts but now plainly see his mistakes. Had the fear of the Lord been imparted in our lives at an early age, my life would have been so different. My choices would have been different. Now that I am an adult and understand it is my responsibility to impart to my loved ones and others this wisdom.

"The fear of the LORD is the beginning of wisdom, and the knowledge of the Holy One is understanding." Proverbs 9:10

Spirit of Excellence
"Whatever you do, do it heartily, as to the Lord and not to men, knowing that from the Lord you will receive the reward of the inheritance, for you serve the Lord Christ." Colossians 3:23-24

This is one of my most favorite scriptures, one that I certainly live by.

As I stated, my dad was very strict and stern. We had to walk a straight line and follow the rules, or else we would experience his anger. So, again I did just enough to get by. He was a drill sergeant and would check to see if we would do our chores correctly and make us do them over if it didn't meet his requirements. Dad was a teacher; he would take the time to show us how it should be done. Therefore, he expected that we would follow his example.

This training helped me in my adult life. However, I found that God takes it to another level. God expects us to do our best in *all* that we do. After I left my dad's home, God sent others to further impart the Spirit of Excellence.

I recall my business school instructor, Ms. Clark, I despised her because she reminded me of my dad. She was very strict and stern. As I reflect, I believe that she was miserable and took it out on us. Anyway, she would dictate letters to the class, our assignment was to transcribe and type the letters to mail.

I would proudly present all my letters and would be disappointed because they would all be returned with a red U, meaning that they were unable to mail because there was perhaps a comma out of place. It would sometimes be the minutest error, nonetheless, unable to mail.

Years later, I now understand that Ms. Clark's assignment was to instill in me the Spirit of Excellence. I appreciate her to this day, and ask God to bless her and her family.

Later, God gave me a pastor that was even harder. I thank God for her life and attribute my writing skills to her. She also was very strict and stern and half doing an assignment was not good enough.

My grandchildren, hopefully, will appreciate me because I, too am a hard taskmaster. I can't help it because it has been instilled in me.

Here, the wonderful thing about living our lives to the best of our ability is that our reward is going to come from God. Wow, how good is that? Executing every assignment with our whole heart as unto the Lord is a major key to success. Being sloppy, without care or diligence is not pleasing to God.

Chess Move!
I have found that sometimes I'm asked to do something that I don't want to do, but I do it anyway. My attitude is that I'm doing this for God and not man because my reward is coming from the Master and not a mere man. It really makes all the difference.

God never forgets your labor of love. He is the Best Boss!!

Who Do You Live to Please?
"For do I now persuade men, or God? Or do I seek to please men? For if I still pleased men, I would not be a bondservant of Christ." Galatians 1:10

All throughout each day, we must make decisions regarding who we are serving. Many are unknowingly living life as a man pleaser. Lives are consumed with pleasing men and no thought of pleasing God.

Each day, I purpose to live a life that is pleasing to God. Sometimes, throughout the day, I am truly challenged to choose God. Who wants to stand out as an oddball? As I get older and have walked this Christian life for a while, it gets easier to say *no* when the world is saying *yes*.

Wisdom is making the right decisions based on the Word of God and the fear of the Lord. Each day, we have to choose between being wise or foolish. For years, I had walked in foolishness and made many bad decisions. In this new life, I am determined to walk in the Wisdom of God.

Giving Tithes and Offerings is a Key to Wealth
This was a real challenge, first of all, the concept was entirely new to both of us. Plus, we were barely making our ends meet. My husband was selling insurance, which barely paid our rent. Many times, we would go to a buffet lunch and eat enough for two days, just joking. I am ashamed to admit that I would steal chicken wings for dinner.

Of course, I repented. It is good not to forget how far we have come. I no longer eat chicken, but I don't have to steal to eat. Hallelujah!!

Let's Talk About Giving and Kill that Selfish, Greedy Demon once & for all. "...And remember the words of the Lord Jesus, He said, *"It is more blessed to give than to receive."* Acts 20:35

We will fight for our money! I had heard so many awful things about pastors using our money for their selfish gain. We both were a little hesitant to give, but we decided to put God to a test. We now faithfully tithe and give offerings. We are blessed because of our giving.

Being a Good Steward
"His lord said to him, *"Well done, good and faithful, you were faithful over a few things, I will make you ruler over many things. Enter into the joy of your lord."* Matthew 25:21

I believe God tests us to see how faithful we will be in the care of what He gives us. When He sees that we can be trusted, He gives us more. When we first get the new car, we wash it every day. Now that the newness has worn off and it is just transportation, we don't wash it, and it's full of junk. Or how about that new house or apartment? We were praising the Lord for it, now it is junky and filthy. But yet, we are praying for a new car and house. Why would God answer your prayers and give you more and you aren't faithful with the little?

Being a good steward of your money is important also. If we are wasteful, stingy, not paying tithes or giving offering with a small amount of money, it is going to be impossible to manage large sums of money. It would be just more money to waste.

I believe that God puts money into the hands of those that will be faithful, and will be obedient to use the money as God planned. It would be wonderful to be God's banker. When God has a big or small project, and funding is needed, He provides through you.

Many are blessed to be a blessing. I have a friend, June that is a millionaire. June believes that 100 % of her income is God's. Some believe that after you give the 10%, then 90% belongs them. Perhaps, her understanding is the reason that God has entrusted her with millions.

Be a Giver
"And remember the words of the Lord Jesus, that." He said, *"It is more blessed to give than to receive."* Acts 20:35

When I first got saved, and I heard this scripture, I didn't understand it. It is just the opposite of the way that I thought all my life. I loved to receive and wasn't big on giving. God's ways are so different from ours. This is the reason that we must learn His ways and will in order to excel in this life. It is a supernatural principle.

Whenever, and whatever you give you will receive it back. It's like you can't out-give God giving back to you. God has proven it to me time and time again. He has instructed me to give a certain amount of money as an offering in church. Sometimes, I'm reluctant, but I give it anyway out of obedience. I will always notice a joy and peace when I have allowed God to use me.

Shortly afterward, God always does something special for me and I would know it was because I gave.

My friend, June the millionaire, loves to give, especially in secret. God can tell her to pay a student's tuition without them knowing that it was her. Or she has bought cars for struggling mothers or someone in dire need. She is always being unexpectantly blessed financially. God likes to surprise. After all, the scripture, Ephesian 3:20, "*...He is able to do exceedingly abundantly above all that we ask or think, according to the power that works in us.*" Did you get that? He can and will do more than we imagine. He will blow your mind with His Goodness, especially if you are obedient and learn to give like Sister June. Her motto is to not let your right hand know what the left hand is doing.

I actually witnessed her going from being broke to becoming a millionaire. Even though she was in debt, she would give large offerings to her church. Shortly afterward, God would give her a business idea. She would do exactly what God said, and the money started to flow into her house. I watched her change zip codes several times. The last house she moved into, she actually paid for it with cash. All because Sister June is obedient and a giver.

Be Quick to Forgive
Unforgiveness can kill you!! That's right!! Some people are suffering major illnesses because of unforgiveness which has turned into a root of bitterness.

How can you know when you have unforgiveness in your heart? Answer these questions: Does the mention of someone's name brings negative emotions and stir up unpleasant memories? Do you go out of your way to avoid this person and drudge being in their presence? If you answered, yes to these questions, there might be unforgiveness in your heart.

Unforgiveness can be a silent killer; since many times, a person can unknowingly have unforgiveness or are in denial.

I have found that deep resentment, comes as a result of repeated offenses. Being in a toxic relationship is very harmful.

I have been in a couple of relationships that ended up in a bitter state. It took years of emotional abuse to get to that point. The process of forgiveness didn't come overnight. I realized that for my sake, I had to forgive both of these people. I was challenged because initially, I didn't want to forgive them. I wanted to hold on to the grudge, not realizing that I was harming myself not the person.

Yes, you are harming yourself! The person has gone on with their life and may not even know how much power they have over you. That's right, they have power over you if they can enter a room and you feel like dying. That's too much power.

When I realized that these were not good relationships, I discontinued the daily interactions. Even today, I'm only in their presence when it's necessary. They are not my favorite people to be around. The difference now is that I do love them but at a distance. I don't dread being around them, but the conversation is short and sweet. Because I know that they have the capacity to cut me at the core of my heart. I would compare these individuals to the powerful pieces in the game of Chess.

Well, I have learned how to maneuver around them. I don't have to have them in my life daily.

How did I get over my dislike for them? As I said, it is a process. It doesn't have to take long; you just have to be willing to forgive. I recall one situation; the forgiveness was instant! I actually despised this person one day and the next day, loved them dearly. Only God can touch your heart like that.

Other times, it took years. I would think I was over a person until their name was mentioned. I was fine until these negative emotions were stirred up.

At church, whenever the topic is forgiveness, and there is a call to the altar for prayer, I would feel the tug of the Holy Spirit to go up for prayer. How many times? I thought I was OK. But I learned that there were layers of hurt. It was like an onion, just pulling back the layers, one layer at a time.

Chess Move!
Regardless of the process, begin today to ask God to show you what's in your heart. If there is unforgiveness, ask for a forgiving heart, repent and ask God to cleanse your heart.

It is such a liberating feeling to have a clean heart and to love everybody. I honestly love my enemies and all those that have done me wrong. I pray that God would bless them mightily.

I periodically ask God to check my heart to make sure that I'm pure. *"Blessed is the pure in heart, for they shall see God."* Matthew 5:8

"Fervently pray for your enemies and really desire to see them blessed. Hopefully, these individuals have changed their ways, all things are possible." Mark 9:23

"But I say to you, love your enemies, bless those who curse you, do good to those who hate you, and pray for those who spitefully use you and persecute you." Matthew 5:44

Don't forget, if you want God's Forgiveness, you must forgive others.

Be Kind
"But the fruit of the Spirit is love, joy, peace, longsuffering, kindness, goodness, faithfulness..." Galatians 5.22

Let's talk about kindness, brotherly kindness. As I mentioned, I realized that I naturally had a kind and giving spirit. I would give my last until I got tired of people misusing me and taking me for granted. I tried to harden up and stopped helping people. It was very unnatural for me, but I thought I had to put up this wall of protection, which may be the state of most people.

Again, we see God's ways are so different from ours. Kindness is one of God's fruits or characteristics. Now, I understand that God made me to be kind and giving because I'm made in His image. However, being kind can have its adverse side.

It's always good to seek God's will in every decision. In a case that God is dealing with a person by chastening them and they are experiencing hardship, this is not the time for you to step in and be God by rescuing them because of your kindness. Caution, if you continually get in God's way by stepping in with your kindness, He will remove you!!

Imagine being wealthy, kind, and giving!! How would you handle all the people that will approach you for financial help because they know you have it? First of all, you have to pray about it. When it comes to relatives, Sister June says when God gives her the ok to help them, she doesn't loan it but gives it to them not expecting repayment.

The Holy Spirit that now dwells in you is so Sweet and Kind. The more that you soften up and allow the Holy Spirit the liberty to be kind, the more natural it becomes. Ideas will come into your minds about kind and thoughtful things you can do for your brothers and sisters.

Chess Move
Kindness isn't a waiting game where you wait until someone is kind to you and then you respond kindly. Be the first to be kind in every situation. Remember, you will reap what you sow.

When you are kind to someone that has mistreated you, guess what, you win. They see the God that is in you because it isn't natural to react in such a way. The Bible says, "*If your enemy is hungry, feed him. If he is thirsty, give him a drink. For in so doing, you will heap coals of fire on his head.*" Romans 12:20 Don't you agree it is supernatural. The results can turn a situation totally around. Being kind to people in this cold world will bring people to the light. Just like God was kind and loved on you and me when we weren't thinking about Him. Remember, we only talked to Him when we needed something. His loving kindness is what drew us to Him!

"The LORD appeared to us in the past, saying, "I have loved you with an everlasting love, I have drawn you with unfailing kindness." Jeremiah 31:3

How do we allow God's Kindness to flow through us? I'm glad that you asked.

The Holy Spirit is Our Guide
Yielding to the leading of the Holy Spirit is the key. The more that you yield, the more natural and first nature that it becomes. It becomes natural to lend a helping hand or volunteer to assist a person in need.

I think it is treating people the way that you want to be treated. During the season that God was unhardening my heart, I would miss a lot of opportunities to be kind. The Holy Spirit would always bring to my remembrance the incident. I would repent and determine to be more attentive to His leadings.

One day, I was browsing in a resale shop. The atmosphere was very pleasant, relaxing music, not too crowded. It was one of the cashiers' birthday, and she made sure everyone that came in knew it. As I continued to shop, the Holy Spirit told me to buy her a gift. So, I found a gift bag and proceeded to pick little trinkets to give to her. When I got to the counter, I asked her if she liked several of the items, she said yes. I put everything back in the gift bag, handed it to her and said "Happy Birthday!" She began to cry and others that witnessed the Kindness of God. We were all blessed by my obedience. The gift was inexpensive, but it was something that I would never have thought of. I returned to the store about a month later, and she still remembered me and told me that she used the items to decorate her new home.

1987 A.D.
My first experience as a legitimate
Business Owner
I had returned to work with my family; my dad had decided to venture into the dry-cleaning business. The business wasn't turning a profit when my dad surprised me by giving the business to me. I gladly accepted the challenge since it was during the summer when business is slow and didn't have any established clientele.

I prayed and asked God what to do? I hired my daughter to handle the counter and a seamstress to do alterations. I took on a job as a maid with a service in the suburbs to help cover the expenses. I began to advertise that we did professional work. Slowly we started to build the business; we had returning customers because of the quality work and the pleasant customer service.

Everyone was getting paid except me. I had to buy plastic clothes bags, hangers, pins, etc. There was more to this business than I had imagined. Every time that I had extra money, I heard the Holy Spirit's reminder to take care of the legal affairs and put the business in my name. I kept ignoring His instructions, after all, this is my dad.

Well, we survived the summer, fall came, and business began picking up, by winter, the business was turning a big profit!! One day, my dad stopped by, and he saw all the clothes that had come in to be dry cleaned. The next day, he returned and took the business back. He made an excuse, but I couldn't argue because legally it was still his business. Needless to say, I was very hurt but I learned a very valuable lesson.

1988 A.D.
Maid Service Established
People would often ask me to clean their home, especially when they visited my home. I like a clean house, not that I love cleaning, but I like the finished product.

One day, my pastor asked me to clean her house, I was offended. I thought, I desire to hire a maid not to be one! That was a bad attitude, wasn't it? Anyway, months later, one of my friends told me that she had gotten a revelation regarding gifts and talents. She said that God had given each of us an innate gift, the ability to perform a duty with excellence without being taught. This innate gift provided by our Creator can be used to provide income. I begin to think of my skill of house cleaning as being a gift.

One day, as I was cleaning the restroom at the church (I volunteered several days a week), I heard that small, still voice saying, "Don't just clean but give it the professional touch that you learned while working as a maid." I slowed down and put the finishing touches on the job. Then I heard the Holy Spirit say, "Maid service, maid service, maid service..." until I got it. I had been praying for another business; this made sense. I had gained experience while working as a maid. I was confident that I could do this!

When my pastor came into the office, I told her that I was going to start a maid service. She was not shocked because she knew all along that I had a gift to clean.

I almost missed God because of my pride. I thank Him that He was patient with me.

She encouraged me by saying that a lot of pastors needed the cleaning services of a reputable company. She then prayed with me.

Chess Move!
Can You Keep a Secret?
It was really hard to not tell my husband about my experience in the church bathroom. I chose not to tell him about my idea

because I didn't want him to possibly ridicule and speak doubt. I needed words of faith and more instructions.

You can't always share everything that the Holy Spirit is telling you.

I listened for my next instructions for months; there was no one else that I could talk about this with. I didn't know anyone that had a maid service. One day, I was back at the church volunteering when Sister Sharpe, a new member of the church stopped by the church office unannounced. She wanted to take Sister Elizabeth and me out to lunch. She had noticed how faithfully we served and wanted to show her appreciation. While at lunch, I felt comfortable enough to share my vision of owning a maid service. Sister Sharpe was so excited and started to share her experiences with her maid service. Wow, finally I saw some light. We decided to go by her condo to get a brochure that her maids had left. Eventually, we ended up back at the church, Sister Sharpe suddenly turned to me, as if a bolt of lightning had struck her, and asked if I wanted to clean her condo, her fiancee's, and the pastor's home next week. I was speechless, all I could do was nod my head, yes. "Really, God, You were silent all this time, and in one day, I have three jobs and clients!!"

I was truly excited but when I got home and was sitting alone, the fear started talking, questions about how I was going to do it, and the fact that I didn't have supplies, every negative thought began to bombard me.

Chess Move

Finally, I heard the Holy Spirit speak in a quiet, still voice that instantly calmed me down. He said, "Go to Kmart and purchase supplies as if you were cleaning your house. Rent a carpet shampooer and do what you know to do." I was obedient; I started the maid service with $20 worth of supplies.

But wait, God wasn't finished yet! The next day was gloomy, and I was a little tired from all the excitement from the previous day. It was very hard to press my way to the church office. However, the thought of the unfinished work gave me the motivation to persevere. I was a little disappointed to find that no other volunteers had shown up to give a helping hand.

I sat down at my desk and resolved that I would complete my assignment with or without help. I recalled my favorite scripture, *"Whatsoever you do, do it heartily, as to the LORD and not to men, knowing that from the LORD you will receive the reward of the inheritance, for you serve the LORD Christ."* Colossians 3:23-24

Suddenly, the door opened, and guess who walks in? No, not Sister Elizabeth but Sister Sharpe. She was more excited than she was the day before. She was almost out of breath when she began to tell me that she had a dream last night and God gave her the name of my business. Last night, after getting my cleaning supplies, I had asked God, what was the name?

She told me the name; I absolutely loved it. Only God could have given her that name. She said that whenever I would say the name of the business, I would be reminded that I was a servant. I thought, well that will help me to remain humble, no more prideful attitudes. She said I was a doulos (Greek, for servant, slave, entirely at the disposal of a master). A servant for Jesus, I don't mind.

She then went into her purse and pulled out her checkbook. My eyes bucked wide open; I was no longer tired and sleepy. The check was already filled out except my last name. She asked my last name, wrote in the blank space, and handed me the check!!

She proceeded to advise me to go right away to register my business and take care of all the necessary paperwork. I knew that was God because He didn't want me to make the same mistake that I had made with the dry cleaner that He had given me.

I finally told my husband, he didn't speak any doubt, and he didn't say anything to encourage me. My first job was Sister Sharpe; it was an eight-hour job. I charged her the same rate as her former maids had charged. Oh, by the way, they were fired, and I was hired. Favor sometimes isn't fair. I was tired, but it was so fulfilling working for myself.

My next job was the Pastor's home, now that was a challenge but I was richly compensated for my days of labor.

Finally, the next week I cleaned her fiance's apartment, he was so pleased with the extra touches. He had a window that was without curtains, I found a curtain that would fit perfectly but didn't have a rod. The thought came to go to the basement, I walked right to a dark corner, and there was a rod that fitted perfectly. I couldn't believe how God had lead me to complete the job far above what the client had requested or expected.

Mr. Jack, her fiancé, was so pleased that he told a friend about my services. He also hired me to service his home. The rest is history; I have been in the maid service business for almost 30 years. My husband, daughter, and other family members have worked with me. We hired 100s of people, some right out of prison, single moms, students, seniors, etc.

When I think about all the clients' homes that we have provided service for over thirty years, I want to cry.

We had the privilege of providing home care to clients while they lived their last days. At one point, quite a few of them were dying; I asked God why? He said that he had opened that door for us to minister salvation to them before they made their transition. I began to understand that our business was actually a ministry.

Flashbacks!
If you don't mind, I have three stories that I would love to share.

Sometimes family members would seek our service because a loved one was unable to care for their home due to illness, or other circumstances. I never knew what to expect when I went on a consultation. This particular day, I asked our secretary to accompany me. What we saw was unbelievable! The mother was very ill and unable to care for herself or her two daughters. I can't describe the living conditions; I was so glad that I had a witness and was not alone.

She hired us to cook and clean on a regular basis. We prayed for her each day that we came and cooked whatever food that she had an appetite for. She hadn't been eating, just consuming medicine and waiting to die.

During the months that we served her, we witnessed a miracle. We learned that she was a backslider and once served the Lord. She had gotten off on the wrong road and began to use drugs which led to the deterioration of her body. We watched her come back from the dead; she was full of life. Her family was so appreciative of our service.

I noticed that the better she felt, the more she craved the things of the world. We encouraged her to get back into church but she wanted to go out to party. One day, she asked me if I would become guardian of her girls. I prayed about it but told her no, mainly because they had an adult sister.

I had grown very fond of her daughters, Jala & Christine. The girls didn't get along with each other and would always fuss and fight. So, to give the mother a break, on the weekends, I would take one of them home with me.

One Sunday evening, I was taking Jala back home to prepare for school. When we got there, an ambulance was there and they were taking the mother out in a wheel chair. I introduced myself to the EMS drivers as the maid. They told me to follow them to the hospital because she had already died, that they had carried her out in a chair to not alarm the neighbors and her children.

That was a trying week, helping the family prepare to bury their loved one. After I performed my obligations, I tearfully said my good byes. The little girls went to live with their sister and her family. I have lost contact with them but often wonder how things are with them.

My second story is brief but amazing. One day, an elderly lady accidentally called my phone number. She was desperately trying to contact her brother because she was having difficulty breathing. I prayed for her and she began to feel better. She thanked me and hung up the phone.

The next week, I called her to see how she was doing. She was good, and asked if I could bring her food on the weekends. She was on a government program that brought food during the week but not on weekends. I agreed.

The first time I went to meet her; I was shocked when she opened the door. She looked exactly like my deceased aunt. I thought to run and not enter her home, it was like seeing a ghost. I'm glad that I mustered up the courage to go in to meet her. She was a very nice but lonesome woman. I prayed that my life would not end up like hers. Nonetheless, I became her friend.

One week, I called and didn't get an answer. I was alarmed because this was very unusual since she seldom went out. The second week, still no answer. Finally, I thought about her brother and called variations of my phone number until I finally reached him. He was surprised that she had a friend that cared and reluctantly told me that she had died and the funeral was the next day.

I attended her funeral to pay my last respect. It was short and sweet, with about 20 people in attendance. I was so sad because I never got the chance to hear her story. I did talk to her about Jesus and believe that she is in heaven looking down at me.

I could write a separate book, *Encounters of a Maid*, there were so many great people that I had the pleasure of serving. This next encounter was the most life changing, I share this story more than any of the rest.

I had received a call from a pastor requesting an estimate for maid service, she was referred by another pastor. At the time, I was no longer taking on any personal clients; any new clients were being cared for by our staff which had grown to ten.

The consultation went very well, I actually fell in love with Pastor Jane. I thought that she would be a perfect mentor; she was living a life that I envisioned for myself. She seemed to be a happy wife and mother, her home was beautifully decorated, white carpet throughout (a bit much for my taste), everything had its place. She glowed as she talked about her busy yet fulfilling work as co-pastor alongside her dad, Pastor Jacob.

At the conclusion of the walk-through, I was amazed because her home was perfect. But then, I thought that I hadn't looked into the oven, certainty that was it, the oven always needs cleaning. Surprise, the oven was spotless. So finally, I asked her, why she called me? She replied, that she needed my help to maintain her home exactly the way that it is. She insisted that she only wanted me to care for her home, and for me to get back with her with my cost.

Well, she was quite demanding, but I told her I would pray. On the way out of the door, I felt impressed to pray for her. I struggled with the nudging of the Holy Spirit for several reasons. One, this is a pastor and at the time, I wasn't a minister. Two, I had been there for an hour, had tea and been there too long already. Three, her son came home and wanted his mom's attention. So, I felt justified in my ignoring the Holy Spirit and sheepishly left.

That was the last time that I saw her in the natural; actually, I visualize her right now as I'm sitting here typing this… she was so beautiful!!

Well, the pastor that had referred her to me called a couple of days later. He started off by asking if I was sitting down, and if I wasn't, to have a seat because he had shocking news for me.

The beautiful Pastor Jane was no longer with us. She had been murdered! Someone had come into her home and mutilated her. The pastor said that all the white carpet was a bloody mess.

I immediately thought about my battle at her side door... I should have prayed for her. If I had, she might be with us today. I will only know when I get to heaven and see her face to face.

As I was typing this, the revelation came that what looks perfect isn't always perfect. She may have been a troubled woman, and my praying for her may have made a difference.

For years, I would come to tears and resented my disobedience. Now, I can share that story with a repented and forgiving heart. I have repented and strive daily to be obedient to God and not to argue and debate when I'm given an uncomfortable assignment. I realize that I have an awesome call and responsibility to God's people. You see, we all are important to God and He has a need for every one of us.

Eyes on You
I have silver hair (that's sounds better than grey hair), not by choice but because of obedience to GOD. My hair color of choice was blonde or bright red during my years living the low life. I have pictures of myself with blonde hair working in the church office. I held on to my right to choose my hair color until one day the Holy Spirit spoke to me.

I clearly heard Him say that the young women need to see grey headed women. No explanation, just a fact. I didn't argue; I just made the decision that I would no longer dye my hair. It has been a journey since I was in my 30s. I was really surprised that as the blonde grew out, this beautiful silver began to surface. It was a mixture, salt and pepper; I absolutely loved it.

Everyone had their opinion of my hair color; some said I was too young for silver; others loved it. All I know is that it does what it needs to do, which is to draw attention to me. The same way the blonde did when I walked the streets as a prostitute.

My hair is an attention getter wherever I go, one day I drove up to the grocery store parking lot, and two ladies were raving over my hair. I got out of the car, and they complimented me. I seized the opportunity to witness to them about God, and exchanged contact information. I followed up with them with a text inviting them to meet for coffee or tea at the local shop in that area.

When I got into the grocery store, a young man, for a moment, thought that I was his aunt who has silver hair. We struck up a conversation, and he invited me to his family's church. We exchanged contact information, of course, I followed up with him too, inviting him to meet at a local coffee shop.

People are watching us wherever we go. Our families are watching us as we continue to lift up the Name of Jesus. My family was waiting for years for me to revert to my former lifestyle. Many years have passed, I believe that they are convinced that I have really changed.

Now, they are watching for the manifestations of those things that I have spoken and claimed by faith. One being my wealth, total deliverance from the yoke of poverty. I believe the Word of God that proclaims, *"Beloved, I pray that you may prosper in all things and be in health, just as your soul prospers."* 3 John 1:2. I certainly agree with John's prayer.

Jesus came to earth, suffered, died, and rose again so that we can have abundant life. The enemy, the thief's main objective is to keep us from seeing the manifestation. The thief doesn't want God's Glory in our lives because many will begin to follow us.

These are the words of Jesus, not John's, *"The thief does not come except to steal, and to kill, and to destroy. I have come that they may have life, and that they may have it more abundantly."* John 10:10. I don't want you to miss this, Jesus came to give us life, that would be good enough, but He added that He desires for us to live a more abundant life. Wow, what does that look like? That is exactly what God desires to do in our lives, to show up and show off for the world to see.

When I walk into a room, I must be mindful that eyes are on me. Even though we don't see people gazing, just know that eyes are on you. So, I make sure that they get a good eye full. Before I leave the house, I make sure that my appearance is great. If I am having a bad hair day, I put on a hat, wig, or scarf;

there is no excuse for being ungroomed. Remember, you are representing the King of Glory. Ask the Holy Spirit's opinion as you dress and get His final approval before stepping out into the world.

Enter a room with a smile and a greeting. When I sit down, I greet those that are seated near me. For one, you have just entered into their space; you have to be the first to show yourself friendly. People will sit next to one another for hours and never speak one word to each other. How sad to ride on a bus, train or any mode of transportation and not say hello. Remember, these are your brothers and sisters; we are a part of God's Family.

What do you do when God has blessed you? Do you keep it a secret; of course not!! The question is how do you give God the Glory publicly? I have been using Facebook… my family members are all on social media. We may not talk, but we keep up with our lives via the internet. This is truly a different kind of world; you have to keep up.

Chess Move
For instance, my car broke down, and I needed a new car. I posted the need and the fact that I was waiting for God to show up and show out. I came back a couple of weeks later with a picture of my new vehicle that God had provided! I was very careful to give Glory to God even though he had used my husband to find the car and to secure the finances to pay for the car.

Going back to John's prayer, 3 John 2:2, he also asked that we be in health. The enemy desires for us to be sick and full of disease. But Jesus took a beating before being hung on the cross, for mankind to be whole. "*...by His stripes* (blows that He endured) *we are healed."* Isaiah 53:5. God is glorified whenever a person testifies to the victory of a sickness, disease, poverty, lack, restored family, etc.

People are watching you, let them see Jesus in you. Let them hear Jesus when you speak words of kindness and wisdom. Let's not miss any opportunities to brag about the Goodness of our God!!

The Word of God Beats Cancer!
One day, I got that phone call that I never wanted to get from my doctor. I can remember it as if it was yesterday... I was sitting at my desk when my doctor called. I had taken some test that showed some abnormalities in my cervix. I had been waiting for the results of the second round of tests. He said that I needed to come into the office for the results, but I persuaded him to tell me over the phone. When he told me that I positively tested for cervical cancer, my heart literally stopped. He asked me if I was alright. I said, yes, and hung up.

I was glad that I wasn't alone when that call came. I just sat there for the longest until I heard the voice of God. These were His instructions: to never say or think that you have cervical cancer. Whenever I discussed the matter, I was to say, "I was diagnosed with cervical cancer." I was only to tell three people about the diagnosis other than my husband. I was to ask them to pray with me and for them to not tell people of the diagnosis.

If I had gotten on Facebook live and broadcasted the diagnosis, things would have gone very differently. People would have been saying, "Bettie has cervical cancer," which is very different from saying Bettie has been diagnosed with cervical cancer.

Chess Move
I never received it; whatever they saw was passing through my system. I was not taking ownership of it. So, I told my friend, Brenda who is a prayer warrior, the gentleman that was present when I got the call, and an elder at our church. I wasn't led to go to the pastor. During this time, I was a student at our church's school of ministry. It was a challenge to study during this time; my mind was, of course, being attacked daily.

Our classes were on Saturday, after class one day, I sat down to tell the elder. She listened intently, after I had finished, she just put her hand on my forehead and said, "God, give her peace in her mind." That was it, that was all that she said. I went back to my seat, and I can honestly say that I had peace of mind after that prayer. I was able to concentrate on my studies; I realized that this was a distraction and I had the victory already.

I had one scripture that I would quote all throughout the day, especially when my mind would begin to dwell on the diagnosis. Psalms 118:17 *"I shall not die, but live, and declare the works of the LORD."* Here I am, many years later cancer free! When I went back to the doctor to discuss the treatment that they were prescribing, he asked that my husband be present.

I am so grateful, for the doctor's thoroughness because he asked for another test. You guessed it; it came back negative!! There was no cancerous cells found in my body!! ONLY GOD!! It was just a distraction, I finished the school of ministry and was ordained. I thank God for giving me the wisdom to sit still to hear what He had to say about the matter.

I have shared this life-changing scripture with many people since. Our grandson was afflicted with Leukemia at the age of three. We all agreed to speak that *he would not die but live to declare the glory of the Lord.* He is now a strong, healthy young man with greater potential and destiny.

I believe sickness is like a piece of lint that can attach itself to your clothes. It is there but it doesn't belong to you, but once one claims it, then it becomes a part of that person.

I shudder when I hear people say my cancer, my diabetes, my heart disease, etc. They have taken ownership of the sickness and disease instead of quoting scriptures due to a lack of knowledge. There are so many healing scriptures in the Bible. Again, our words can create or destroy. I will add a list of healing scriptures at the end of this diary. Please, keep this book as a reference because you don't know when the enemy will attack you, a family member or close loved ones with sickness.

Praise Break!

One night at bible study, the Holy Spirit changed the order of service. It was kind of funny, the pastor tried to move on with his lesson, but the Spirit of God overtook him. He attempted several times to regain control of the service, but the people had entered into worship, and there was no turning back.

Finally, the pastor yielded and allowed the Holy Spirit to have His way. The pastor actually led us into worship. He repeatedly urged us to forget about the person next to us and focus on how far God has brought us. I began to reflect on God's Goodness and Mercy. As I reflected on this book and my testimony, I thought that this would be a good place to have a praise break, please join me by reflecting on your past. We can become consumed and focused on the present, future goals and plans that we forget where we've come from.

Chess Move!

Thank you, Father for loving me enough to send your son, Jesus to redeem me from my sins. Thank you, Father for making a way of escape for all your children and me. Thank you that the price of sin was paid for us. I realize that the wages for my sin was death, but Jesus paid it for me. Thank you, Jesus for being obedient to the point of death, even though you didn't have to do it. Thank you, Jesus for your love of the Father, that you suffered and died for me.

Now that you have risen and are now seated at the right side of the Father, I thank you that you're constantly praying for us 24 hours a day. I appreciate that you didn't leave us comfortless, but left the Holy Spirit here to be our Comforter and Guide.

Thank you, Holy Spirit, that you are consistently beside me to watch over me. Thank you that you convict me when I am wrong. Thank you for your gentle touch when I am going the wrong way due to ignorance or disobedience. Thank you, Holy Spirit for reminding me of the words and instructions already spoken to me. Thank you, Holy Spirit for teaching me all things that pertain to life and godliness. You know that I don't know how to live a life that is pleasing to God, the Father. You know the reason that I was placed on this earth. Thank you, Holy Spirit for orchestrating my path that I will be at the right place at the right time with the right attitude.

Chapter 6
Prostitution to Preaching
I Accepted the Call

"Therefore, if anyone cleanses himself from the latter, he will be a vessel for honor, sanctified and useful for the Master, prepared for every good work." 2 Timothy 2:21

I didn't see it coming; I never had a desire to preach. Even though when my siblings and I would play together, I would always be the teacher when we played school or the pastor when we played church. Again, I was the oldest of five siblings, so I was always the leader. Here it is, years later and that is exactly what my passion is, to teach and preach!

From day one of my salvation, Friday, March 13, 1979, I was a student. It bears repeating, *I would take notes* at each service or Bible study. When I got home, *I would go over my notes* and preach the message the next day to anyone that would listen.

One Sunday, my pastor was talking about evangelizing our families. She said that it is good to minister to those outsiders but to not forget about our family members. She made a statement that hit my very core; she said that it would be a shame for our family members to die at the age of 80 and 90 and never have accepted Jesus as their savior.

I thought about my grandfather, who was over 100 years old. I hadn't seen him in a while; he lived in Mississippi on the family homestead. Once upon a time, he was very tall. The last time that I saw him, he walked bent over because of the curve in his back. He had a good sense of humor, always making us laugh. I have few but fond memories of my grandfather, Oliver.

The thought of my grandfather going to hell really upset me. I left the church with the determination to make sure that my grandfather was ready to meet his Maker.

When I got home, I called my dad and told him about the message and my desire to go and visit his dad. I was surprised when he made a sigh of relief. He had been thinking about his dad and felt the need to go to visit him to make sure that he was being taken care of. My Uncle Sylvester was his caregiver. My dad was self-employed, and this was his peak season and felt that he couldn't take off from work. So, he offered to pay for my transportation there and spending cash. I decided to go on the train, which was my first time.

I had a wonderful, peaceful train ride back to my birthplace. When I arrived, I was surprised at how much my grandfather had deteriorated. He was senile and would sit talking to himself. He was no longer humorous, yet he was still a joy to sit with. He was at peace with himself in his own world. I noticed that he would occasionally snap back into reality and would be able to have a conversation. As my mission trip was coming to an end, I was getting concerned that I would not have an opportunity to minister to my grandfather. There was always someone else present when granddad had those brief moments of clear thoughts.

Chess Move
You know our God, He made a Way. On my last morning, granddad woke up with his full mind. He was his old self, telling jokes and making me laugh. I knew that I had to move fast, so I asked him, "Do you know if you would go to heaven or hell when you died?" He stared at me with piercing eyes totally sober, laying all jokes aside, he said that he didn't know. I replied that he could know for sure that he was going to heaven.

His eyes bulged, and he said, "Sho nuff!" which he was famous for saying. I proceeded to share the Gospel with him and lead him through the sinner's prayer (which is at the end of this book). His eyes glistened with tears as he repented of his life of sin and accepted Jesus as His Lord and Savior. I shouted, my mission was accomplished!! I was relieved of the burden of granddad's salvation.

My granddad lived a few more months; he was 102 years old when he passed. When I received the news, I could rest assured that he was in Heaven with Jesus.

My dad and my eldest brother were making plans to attend the funeral. I wasn't planning on going until God spoke that I needed to be on the program to give my granddad's testimony of how he had accepted Jesus at the age of 101 which would comfort his large family.

I called to Mississippi and asked to be put on the program. I didn't tell my father or brother. I carried my Bibles and studied material to prepare because I felt that there was more that He wanted to say through me. I was instructed to also share my salvation testimony of how God has raised me up from the low life of prostitution and sin.

I was surprised when I learned that I was to speak just before the pastor's eulogy. When my dad saw my name on the program, he turned to me with amazement and tears. I responded with a smile to comfort him.

I nervously sat on the end seat right behind my dad. I realized that my challenge was even greater than just speaking; I had to first take authority over the depressed atmosphere by offering up praise and welcoming the Holy Spirit to lift my family's sadness and grief so we could celebrate granddad's homegoing.

God is so faithful; He gave me the opening statement as I sat there. As I approached the pulpit, I shouted, "Thank you, Jesus for my Grand Father's 102 years!" I continued to boldly and unashamedly praise our GOD; it seemed that I was alone until finally a few people caught on, then there was a shift and others joined in the praise. The more that we praised, more people began to relax and soak in His Presence. His Presence overshadowed me, and I became confident and focused. I came all the way from Detroit with a message for my family.

I preceded to share my grandfather's and my testimony. When I mentioned that I had gone to the depths of prostitution, my father's face dropped. Later, he told me that I didn't have to give that much information. I assured him that it wasn't his fault and not to take it personal, that it was no reflection on how he had raised me. I took full responsibility for my bad decisions. I really did have to tell my story, yes, it wasn't easy or pleasant. I told it just the way GOD had instructed me, I had my notes, and I made sure that I didn't miss saying anything.

I concluded by asking the family to join me at 12 noon the next day, which was Sunday, at Papa's home under the big Oak tree to hear an important message sent from GOD to our family.

The pastor approached the pulpit as I took my seat; he was still praising God and shaking his head saying, "Wow! Wow!! People were standing up clapping their hands, some were crying and loudly praising God!! It was evident that God's Presence was in the room. It was more than I had expected; God is Faithful, He showed up at my grandpa's homegoing!! The pastor said that I had actually given the eulogy, that I knew my Grandfather, and I had spoken well about him. Since he never met my grandfather, all that he could add was the final remarks and we proceeded to the cemetery.

After the funeral was over, I was amazed at the response of my family members. They actually stood in line to greet and meet me, most for the first time. Many asked if they could speak with me privately at a later time. One cousin said that when I spoke, he felt a burning sensation inside of him. All this was new to me; I really didn't know how to respond.

Recognition of The Call to Preach
Finally, the pastor approached me to ask me about my calling. He asked if I was an evangelist. At that moment, I realized that I was called to preach the gospel of Jesus Christ.

After the funeral, I was invited to preach at another church the following day; I had to refuse because I had asked my family to meet me. I was reeling in shock from the response of the people.

Needless to say; I was up all night preparing for the family meeting. I was staying with a cousin that was a member of the church that hosted the funeral. I asked if I could borrow chairs to put under the oak tree. He said, ok.

Chess Move
The next morning, I got dressed and arrived early. I asked my cousin Jean to park at the end of the driveway so that I could make an easy exit after I had delivered the message from God.

Grandpa's house was in the country with farm land surrounding it on all sides. There was a dirt road at the front of it, so you can see cars approaching before they reached the house. The first ones to arrive had the chairs, they unloaded them but didn't place them under the tree. My cousins actually doubted that anyone would come, I demanded that they sat the chairs out under the tree.

11:50 am, a caravan of cars, trucks, and vans started parading slowly down the road to the house. My doubting cousins looked at me in disbelief as the chairs were being filled. Every chair was taken, and some had to stand. We handed out paper and pencil to be used to take notes.

I started off by making sure that no outsiders were present; one of my cousins brought a girlfriend, I told him that she couldn't participate in the meeting.

I opened with prayer. I then spoke about Uncle Sylvester, who cared for grandpa during the last years of his life. When I had visited earlier, Uncle Vest spoke of how he felt that his siblings took him for granted.

I asked Uncle Vest to take a seat in the center of his family. I started to talk about love being a verb, that we can say we love a person but our actions actually show it. I used Uncle Vest as an example of how he showed his love to grandpa by caring for him. I asked our family to love on Uncle Vest by expressing their thanks and to bless him financially, if possible. Their response was overwhelming; the Love of God overshadowed the atmosphere under the oak tree.

Next, I talked about our Uncle Neal, who was very dear to me and my siblings. He was my father's brother, same as Uncle Sylvester. We had a close relationship because he lived in our city and visited often. I witnessed my Uncle go from a high paid city worker to a pauper begging for money to buy liquor. Most of the family never met him or were aware of his story. It was important to mention him because many of them were already walking in his footsteps because of the generational family curses, which led me to the next point.

I had everyone's attention; I began to explain what generational curses were. Then I described our family's strong characteristics; go-getters, not your average person, very confident, high achievers with a standard of excellence and people are drawn to us because of our charisma.

All of these characteristics described our Uncle Neal; however, he had some of these generational curses and never was delivered from them.

I told them to get their paper and write down these five curses that have plagued our family for many generations. I explained each one and gave an example and scenario of each one. I had everyone's undivided attention as I went on to assure them that there was help for us.

I talked about Jesus and how He came to destroy the works of the enemy. How we can renounce the curses and accept the freedom that God had provided for us through His Son, Jesus.

I asked them to stand, and I explained that we would pray together, first to ask Jesus to become our Savior. To become born again, to repent of our sins and to ask Jesus into our hearts and permit Him to be Lord of our lives. Then to renounce the curses, one by one and to rebuke the power of Satan from our lives. We now had the power to do so because Jesus was inside of us.

We boldly prayed as a family under the oak tree. We were set free that day under the big oak tree. When we said, amen, they all silently took their seats. It was totally quiet; I looked at my cousin who had driven me and gave her the sign that it was time to make our exit. I knew that I had embarrassed many of them, their feelings were crushed and exposed. Many were secretly committing these acts, and only God and them knew about their actions.

I was later told that after I left, they began to ask one another how many of these curses were present in their lives? They had honest conversations among the various families. Some of those that were present have since passed on. Hopefully, the meeting under the oak tree made a difference in their lives. I pray that the generational curses were brought to a halt that day not to go on to the next generation.

I also pray that the generational blessings have overtaken our family. We are truly a blessed family.

If you desire more information on generational blessings and curses; go to www.google.com, you will find many books and material available for your enlightenment.

Chapter 7
Whoredom to Worship
My Everyday Life as a Queen!

"I tell you, her sins, and they are many, have been forgiven, so she has shown me much love. But a person who is forgiven little shows only little love." Then Jesus said to the woman, "Your sins are forgiven." Luke 7:47-49

My translation: Bettie's sins, and they are many, have been forgiven, so she has shown me much love. But a person who is forgiven little shows only little love." Then Jesus said to Bettie, "Your sins are forgiven."

Yes, my sins were many!
Thank God, I have been given a second chance. I worship God because He reached down and lifted me up out of hell on earth. The enemy thought that he had me. He had surrounded me, every way that I turned, the enemy was there. It was a real-life chess game, and it appeared that I was defeated. But GOD! One day, I was lost, and the next day, my life was changed forever.

Only God can change a person's life. He is our Creator, and He loves us so much that He gave His son, Jesus, who paid the price for our sins. Think about it; we came out of our mothers' womb a sinner because of Adam's sin, mankind was cursed. You don't have to teach a baby to sin; it is a natural instinct. Knowing that the wages of sin is death, God stepped in and devised a plan to pay the penalty for our sins. He didn't have to make a plan of escape for fallen mankind. But because of His Love for us, He did!

I worship God because of who He is and praise Him for what He does. I honor Him as the Almighty God that cares for His Creation. He has shown me how much He loves me; therefore, I want to show Him how much I love and appreciate being given another chance at abundant life and to live the rest of my life as a queen.

No Class to Royalty!

It is as if I have lived two different lives. You couldn't pay me to go back. I often think of the scripture that says if you go back then your life will be seven times worse than it was. Matthew 12:43-45. Which would mean death for me.

I absolutely love my new life, there is no comparison. Yes, it was challenging in the beginning but so worth it.

Over the years since March 13, 1979, I have seen God work miracle after miracle in my life. I have seen Him work miracles all around me. He is truly a miracle working God.

If you don't believe me, just walk with me for seven days. You will see seven days of miracles.

Queens should see miracles every day. If you aren't, perhaps it is because you are not asking for miracles daily or maybe you don't believe that you can receive miracles daily.

Many times, we receive miracles but don't recognize that they are miracles. It is what your perception of miracles are. The first miracle every day is waking up, being able to dress yourself and on and on. When you become grateful for those things that are often taken for granted, you will see even greater miracles.

Having the presence of God in my home, automobile and His Presence by my side daily is a miracle. I can recall the darkness that once surrounded me. Now, I walk in the light; everywhere I go, I take the light, that is a miracle.

"My every need is met, I have more than enough. Jesus did come to give us life more abundantly." John 10:10.

"If you are not living the abundant life, and are just barely getting by, check yourself. It is not God's fault, He desires for you to have the best." James 1.17

It is amazing how He gets my blessings to me, He will use a stranger. I never limit God, nor do I put Him in a box. I tell Him to bless me in whatever way He sees fit for His daughter.

I feel like a Queen sitting on a throne when people come to me for prayer and to ask my advice. Some are strangers that connect with me by way of Facebook and YouTube. I am so honored for the privilege of connecting God's children to Him.

"I am truly proud to be chosen to be a Queen in God's Kingdom. He is the King of Kings and Lord of Lords." Revelation 17:14. *"I am called, chosen and faithful."*

"The thief does not come except to steal, and to kill, and to destroy. I have come that they may have life, and that they may have it more abundantly." Words spoken by Jesus Christ written in the Bible, John Chapter 10 and Verse 10.

Chapter 8
31 Wisdom Keys of a Virtuous Woman
According to Bettie J Rusher

"Her children rise up and call her blessed; her husband also, and he praises her." **Proverbs 31:28**

My husband and children call me a Virtuous Woman! I did not give myself that title because I don't think I have arrived yet. Actually, I think it is a life long journey to be compared to the Woman that we are introduced to in Proverb 31.

Proverbs 31 is "My Most Favorite Chapter" in the entire Bible. Again, being the eldest child, I didn't have the luxury of having an older sibling to show me the way. So, you can imagine when I first read this chapter and was introduced to "The Proverbs 31/Virtuous Woman," I was elated!! I finally had a role model that I could pattern my life after. I have since met many other virtuous women, so I am inspired.

I thank God for including this portrait of the type of woman that He desires for us to be. I'm encouraged when I feel like I'm missing the mark, I realize that it must be attainable or He wouldn't have called us to this high position. Sis, it is a process...

"...being confident of this very thing, that He who has begun a good work in you will complete it until the day of Jesus Christ." Philippians 1:6

I hope these Wisdom Keys assist you on your journey to "Be the Virtuous Woman that you are Called to Be."

1. *Intentionally advance in the Kingdom every day.* If you stand still, you are actually moving backward. Get up every morning with Kingdom Business on your mind. Always be pregnant birthing a project into the earth. *"She also rises while it is yet night, and provides food for her household, and a portion for her maidservants."* Proverbs 31:15

2. *Watch your thoughts.* If you are thinking about a person or situation consistently, which is to worry, be quick to cast that care on the Lord by releasing it with prayer. Tell God all about it in detail. HE is concerned about everything that concerns you. Nothing is too big or small. *"The LORD will perfect that which concerns me; Your mercy, O LORD, endures forever; Do not forsake the works of Your hands."* Psalms 138:8

3. *As you acquire wisdom and knowledge quickly pass it along.* Remember, the information that you receive is not just for you. Writing notes and rehearsing new findings helps you to retain the information. *"She opens her mouth with wisdom, and on her tongue, is the law of kindness."* Proverbs 31.26

4. *The devil will always challenge your victory*, you can't ever forget the lessons learned and what you did to get the victory. Be quick to resort to former weapons.

5. *Never stop learning.* Some of the strategies that you used in your last season may not work in your new season. Always be actively sharpening your game.

6. *Don't be sidetracked by other women.* Our defense guards are up, looking for the enemy to use a male, but he often uses women. Watch and pray regarding all new acquaintances that appear in your life, as well as your significant other and children's lives. *The Prayer of Sanctification:* "Lord, sanctify this new relationship that we will never bring any reproach to You or to each other and that we would be a blessing to one another and never harm. In Jesus' Name."

7. *Be strong and courageous;* be yourself, go with your gut feeling. Do not follow the crowd; follow the beat of the rhythm that you are hearing. *"Strength and honor are her clothing; She shall rejoice in time to come."* Proverbs 31:25

DIARY OF A VIRTUOUS WOMAN

8. *Don't put GOD in a box.* He is too big for your finite mind to figure out and control. I often say, *"Jesus is Lord, all day and every day."* Allow God to be God; He is the Creator and Producer of your life; just follow the script.

9. *Smile as you gracefully enter into a room* of people, know for a fact that *eyes are on you.* Let them see Christ in you. The Anointing of God in you changes the atmosphere. You bring the Light, smile, you are on candid camera!

10. *Be careful how you spend your time* and who you spend it with. Some people are sent to distract and waste your time. *The devil comes to steal, kill, and destroy.* John 10.10. Time is a Gift that is given to you every day. A Virtuous Woman gets up while everyone else is asleep. Kill the flesh that love, love, and loves sleep!

11. *Practice your graceful walk.* Acknowledge that you are a queen and very valuable. Money should not be able to buy you. *Your price is far above rubies.* Proverbs 31:10

12. *Be skillful in executing the Law of Kindness.* Choose your words, tone, and body language when addressing someone. Be slow to speak, quick to listen, and slow to anger. Remember, these are God's Children. *"She opens her mouth with wisdom, and on her tongue, is the law of kindness."* Proverbs 31:26

13. *Wear your crown graciously.* People's lives are enhanced by your presence and the Holy Spirit's anointing that

accompanies you. People are drawn to you and enjoy hearing you talk. Show yourself to be friendly, sweet, and down to earth. Don't cause people to feel belittled in your presence.

14. *Use your ability to manage* multiple businesses and ministries. You should always be working on an assignment. *"I must work the works of Him who sent Me while it is day; the night is coming when no one can work."* John 9:4

15. *Be slow to anger and quick to forgive.* If you are consistently talking about an offense, it may indicate that there may be unforgiveness in your heart. Forgive as God has forgiven you; He doesn't hold it against you. It is as if He casts our sins into the sea. *"He will turn again, he will have compassion upon us; he will subdue our iniquities; and thou wilt cast all their sins into the depths of the sea."* Micah 7:19

16. *Laugh every day.* Intentionally, make this happen. I laugh at my husband's corny jokes; just get it in.

    "A merry heart does good, like medicine, but a broken spirit dries the bones." Proverbs 17:22

17. *Never say; "I'm sorry,"* when apologizing. By definition, a sorry person is an unfortunate, unhappy, wretched, shameful, regrettable or awful person. You are not a sorry person; stop confessing that you are. You are of great worth.

18. *Never say, "I'm broke."* Your Father owns everything you see, every house, car, etc. So how can you, His daughter, be without money? If you lack funds, take responsibility and find out where you are missing the mark. *"The blessing of the LORD makes one rich, and He adds no sorrow with it."* Proverbs 10:22

19. *Ask God to unleash your authentic self.* The woman that's screaming to come out. Pray about everything; what to wear, hairstyle, model of car, etc. Be free to be you! *"I will praise You, for I am fearfully and wonderfully made; marvelous are Your works, and that my soul knows very well."* Psalms 139:14

20. *Care for yourself.* Take responsibility; schedule regular doctor's visits, eat well and exercise, your health is very important. Also, your appearance is what people see, you are representing the King of Kings." The virtuous woman was well dressed and so was her family. *"She is not afraid of snow for her household, for all her household is clothed with scarlet. She makes tapestry for herself, her clothing is fine linen and purple."* Proverbs 31.21-22

21. *Never settle for less* than what you asked God for. It may require patience, but you don't want second best or to receive the counterfeit due to lack of patience or lack of trust.

22. *Get out of your Comfort Zone*, be willing to stretch yourself. It's a first time for everything. Be adventurous, nobody likes to be around a dull, boring person. People will love to ask you, "What you're up to" because they know you always have something going on! Be a Woman of Action!

23. *Don't be a slob.* Clean up, make your home a haven of rest. Does your family love to be there? What would you do if Jesus unexpectedly dropped by?

24. *Be a Giver.* You will reap what you sow. Giving also includes your time. Schedule time on calendar to nurture friends and family relationships. If you have parents, it's very important to spend time with them via phone or visits, have them on your calendar.

25. *You need a pastor* to watch over your soul. Don't look for a church, look for a pastor and then help him in his mission.

26. *Be a good steward of your money.* Pay tithes and give offering, don't forget to pay yourself, save, and invest. Acquire the skill of managing your money. If you are faithful with the little, He will make you ruler over much.

27. *Speak Powerful-Action words every day.* Use positive adjectives. When asked, "How, I'm doing." Most times, I respond, "I'm blessed." My answer is usually shocking to the hearer. It is an acquired habit that is now natural for

DIARY OF A VIRTUOUS WOMAN

me to say. Also, refrain from using the adjective "hate." It is a very powerful word and most time not necessary to use.

28. *Don't be a wimp*, stand up and fight for what you believe and desire. News Flash!! The devil "ain't" going to give you *anything*; you will have to take it by force.

29. *Remain humble*, remember where you come from. Remember, *"Pride goes before destruction, and a haughty spirit before a fall."* Proverbs 16:18. It's a long way down.

30. *Forgive yourself.* There is no condemnation… the devil is an accuser. Don't allow him to bring up your past; God has forgiven you, *now* you do the same and love yourself.

31. *Did you make your bed today?* God loves order. Most People of excellence make their beds every day. Get the wrinkles out, a wonderful way to start your day. Sometimes, I lay my pajamas out, and say out loud, "I'll be back." It gives me something to look forward to at the end of a long day.

"Charm is deceitful and beauty is passing, but a woman who fears the LORD, she shall be praised." Proverbs 31:30

Healing Scriptures
New Living Translation

1. **Exodus 15:26**
   He said, "If you will listen carefully to the voice of the LORD your God and do what is right in his sight, obeying his commands and keeping all his decrees, then I will not make you suffer any of the diseases I sent on the Egyptians; for I am the LORD who heals you."

2. **Exodus 23:25-26**
   "You must serve only the LORD your God. If you do, I will bless you with food and water, and I will protect you from illness. 26 There will be no miscarriages or infertility in your land, and I will give you long, full lives."

3. **Deuteronomy 7:15**
   "And the LORD will protect you from all sickness. He will not let you suffer from the terrible diseases you knew in Egypt, but he will inflict them on all your enemies!"

4. **Psalm 30:2**
   "O LORD my God, I cried to you for help, and you restored my health."

5. **Psalm 103:2-3**
   "Let all that I am praise the LORD; may I never forget the good things he does for me. ³ He forgives all my sins and heals all my diseases."

6. **Psalm 107:20**
   "He sent out his word and healed them, snatching them from the door of death."

7. **Proverbs 3:7-8**
   "Don't be impressed with your own wisdom. Instead, fear the LORD and turn away from evil. ⁸ Then you will have healing for your body and strength for your bones."

8. **Proverbs 4:20-22**
   "My child, pay attention to what I say. Listen carefully to my words. ²¹ Don't lose sight of them. Let them penetrate deep into your heart, ²² for they bring life to those who find them, and healing to their whole body."

9. **Isaiah 53:4-5**
   "Yet it was our weaknesses he carried; it was our sorrows that weighed him down. And we thought his troubles were a punishment from God, a punishment for his own sins! ⁵ But he was pierced for our rebellion, crushed for our sins.

He was beaten so we could be whole. He was whipped so we could be healed."

10. **Isaiah 58:8**
"Then your salvation will come like the dawn, and your wounds will quickly heal. Your godliness will lead you forward, and the glory of the LORD will protect you from behind."

11. **Jeremiah 30:17**
"I will give you back your health and heal your wounds," says the LORD. "For you are called an outcast— 'Jerusalem for whom no one cares.'"

12. **Jeremiah 33:6**
"Nevertheless, the time will come when I will heal Jerusalem's wounds and give it prosperity and true peace."

13. **Ezekiel 34:16**
"I will search for my lost ones who strayed away, and I will bring them safely home again. I will bandage the injured and strengthen the weak. But I will destroy those who are fat and powerful. I will feed them, yes—feed them justice!"

14. **Malachi 4:2**
"But for you who fear my name, the Sun of Righteousness will rise with healing in his wings. And you will go free, leaping with joy like calves let out to pasture."

15. Matthew 9:35

    "Jesus traveled through all the towns and villages of that area, teaching in the synagogues and announcing the Good News about the Kingdom. And he healed every kind of disease and illness."

16. Mark 16:17-18

    These miraculous signs will accompany those who believe: They will cast out demons in my name, and they will speak in new languages. ¹⁸ They will be able to handle snakes with safety, and if they drink anything poisonous, it won't hurt them. They will be able to place their hands on the sick, and they will be healed."

17. Acts 10:38

    "And you know that God anointed Jesus of Nazareth with the Holy Spirit and with power. Then Jesus went around doing good and healing all who were oppressed by the devil, for God was with him."

18. James 5:14-15

    "Are any of you sick? You should call for the elders of the church to come and pray over you, anointing you with oil in the name of the Lord. ¹⁵ Such a prayer offered in faith will heal the sick, and the Lord will make you well. And if you have committed any sins, you will be forgiven."

19. **1 Peter 2:24**
"He personally carried our sins in his body on the cross so that we can be dead to sin and live for what is right. By his wounds you are healed."

20. **3 John 1:2**
"Dear friend, I hope all is well with you and that you are as healthy in body as you are strong in spirit."

21. **Psalms 118:17 Please memorize and confess out loud.**
"I will not die; instead, I will live to tell what the LORD has done."

Prayer for Healing

Father, according to Your Word, Jesus Himself took stripes on His body so that I could be healed. He bore my sicknesses and diseases, and carried my pains when He died on the cross. Therefore, by faith, I receive healing in my body. I believe that I am healed and that I will continue to experience excellent health in my life. Thank You, Lord, for healing me.

In Jesus' Name, Amen.

Our Memory Scripture: Psalms 118:17 NLT

"I shall not die, but live, and declare the works of the LORD"

Acknowledgements

My Christian journey began Friday, March 13, 1979, at Grace Refuge Chapel on the West side of Detroit, Michigan, the late Pastor Veta Hill.

Since that day, countless people have poured into my life. However, in this volume, I pay homage to the spiritual giants that helped to lay a solid foundation of the truth of God's Word into my life.

Pastors Lloyd and Patricia Westley, Ministers Samuel and Gwendolyn Marshall, Bishop Charles and Co-Pastor Mary Middleton, Pastor Sanford McQueen, the late Pastor Leonard Lyons, Pastor Gilbert Vaughn, Bishop Corletta Vaughn, Pastor Caretha Crawford, and Bishop Marvin Winans.

About the Author

Bettie, raised in Detroit, Michigan USA has been married for most of her life. First, as a pregnant teenager forced by her parents to marry. From the ages 19-27, the honor student's life took a sharp curve, down the road of an abusive marriage, illness, addictions, and prostitution.

Thank God, for March 13, 1979, the day that she surrendered to God, and cried out, "What must I do to be saved from this wretched, low life?" JESUS was the answer, and still is!

As an author-minister, Bettie hopes that you, the reader will gain insight and wisdom to avoid some of the pain that she experienced.

Presently, the Power Couple, Ken and Bettie Rusher enjoy quality time with their blended family. They also, love, love, and love to travel, especially cruising.

Bettie is an author of two books, entrepreneur, massage therapist, and ordained minister. She loves God and His Family, after all, we are one family under God!

Bettie J. Rusher wants to hear from you!

For more information about Bettie's other book, GOD HATES DIVORCE, Malachi 2:16 A Wife's Guide To A Successful Marriage, the Heavenly Marriage Series, Volume 1 or to find out how to book Bettie for your next event, contact Bettie @ www.backtoeden.today, or email: bjrusher@gmail.com or leave a voice mail 586.277.1117

Go to website to download Free E-books,
My Go-To Scriptures and
31 Wisdom Keys of a Virtuous Woman
www.backtoeden.today

Please, submit a positive review @ Amazon.com or where you purchased your book.

Thanks, Hugs and Kisses!
Bettie R.

The Sinner's Prayer

"Father, I know that I have broken your laws and my sins have separated me from you. I am truly sorry, and now I want to turn away from my past sinful life toward you. Please forgive me, and help me avoid sinning again.

I believe that your son, Jesus Christ died on the cross for my sins and rose from the dead on the third day. He is alive and hears my prayers. I invite Jesus to become the Lord of my life, to rule and reign in my heart from this day forward. I confess with my mouth that He is now Lord of my Life!

Please send your Holy Spirit to help me obey You, and to do Your will for the rest of my life.

In Jesus' name I pray, Amen."

Made in the USA
Columbia, SC
17 September 2021